Book Three:

Maximum Saints Dream

Inspirational stories and drawings by incarcerated "Maximum Saints" and volunteers at Adams County Detention Facility, Brighton, Colorado.

Yong Hui V. McDonald

"Not all dreams come from God, and not all dreams are about God; however, we can learn about God through our dreams when we ask Him to help us understand them. God loves each of us, so much so that He sent His Son Jesus to die on the cross for our sins. Scriptures tell us 'seek and you shall find, knock and the door shall be opened.' So it is with our dreams. *MAXIMUM SAINTS DREAM*, just like everyone else. When they seek understanding of those dreams by praying to God, God reveals the meaning of the dreams to them. The healing, comfort, and wisdom that God provides are further testimony of His love for us. Our prayer is that you, too, might discover God in this way."
– Michael Goins, Executive Director of Transformation Project
    Prison Ministry and Media representative

"It has been an honor and a privilege to have been a part of this project as one of the editors. The stories from *MAXIMUM SAINTS DREAM* are inspirational. They will encourage readers to restore their lives to God's purpose and educate them to grow spiritually. Anyone who applies the teachings of this book will gain relief, comfort, and spiritual knowledge of how to move forward."
– Sandra Lee Norris, an inmate at ACDF

MAXIMUM SAINTS DREAM

Printed in the United States of America
ISBN: 978-0-9825551-5-6
Cover drawing: Bobbie Michel, an inmate at ACDF
Cover Design: Lynette McClain
McClain Productions, www.mcclainproductions.com
First Printing: January 2010
Second Printing: November 2011
TPPM is a 501(c)(3) nonprofit corporation.
Transformation Project Prison Ministry
5209 Montview Boulevard, Denver, CO 80207
Website: www.maximumsaints.org
Facebook: http://tinyurl.com/yhhcp5g

Adams County Detention Facility inmates have given their consent to use their stories and illustrations in Maximum Saints books. Some authors and artists names have been changed by their request.

All the proceeds from *Maximum Saints* will go to TPPM to distribute more free books and DVDs to prisons and homeless shelters.

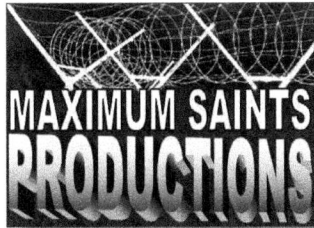

CONTENTS

DEDICATION

I dedicate this book to our Heavenly Father, our Lord Jesus, the Holy Spirit, and to all the incarcerated "Maximum Saints" all over the world whose hearts are serving Christ, saving souls and helping others.

Drawing "Dedication" by Burnie

Maximum saints are not necessarily classified as maximum inmates. I call them maximum saints because they use their gifts to the maximum to help others.

ACKNOWLEDGMENTS

I thank God for my wonderful mother and her prayers. Because of her prayers, God has blessed me in my ministry and I have been so blessed.

My gratitude to all the following generous people who donated their time and gifts to make this book possible:

(1) All the ACDF inmates who contributed their stories.

(2) Drawings: Bobbie Michel and Burnie.

(3) Typing stories: Lori Huff, Maxine Maurie and Laura Lukes Lang.

(4) ACDF editors: Dee Anderson, Shawn Brady, Don Burough, Francesca Cayou, Roland Dequina, Julie Espinosa, Rita Finney, Robert Garcia, Ana Martinez, Stephanie McCoy, Crystal Morgan, Joanne Nobles, Sandra Norris, Andrea L. Putman, Uriah Richards, Julia Roberts, Lupe Rubio, Christian Sandoval, Shannon Schell and Kevin Sullivan.

(5) Volunteers who have helped with editing: Michael Goins, Laura Nokes Lang, Maxine Morarie, Angela Clark, Fletcher McDonald, Mary Oswalt and Helen Sirios.

(6) Art scans: Deputy Sheri Duran, Alvaro Duran and Jim Wickland.

(7) ACDF staff: Sheriff Douglas N. Darr, Captain Roger Engelsman, Melanie Gregory, Technical Services Manager, Mr. Sterritt Fuller, Program Coordinator and all of the Program Department staff.

(8) Donors: The following churches and individuals graciously supported the Transformation Project Prison Ministry through funding: (1) Park Hill United Methodist Church (UMC); (2) Broomfield UMC; (3) Frontier UMC of Cheyenne, Wyoming; (4) Korean-American Christ Central UMC; (5) Fort Lupton UMC; (6) Brighton UMC; (7) First Community UMC in Keenesburg; (8) Westminster UMC; (9) Northglenn UMC; (10) Thornton UMC; (11) Smoky Hill UMC; (12) Jefferson Ave. UMC; (13) Grace UMC; (14) First UMC, Fort Collins; (15) Peoples UMC, Colorado Springs; (16) Stratmoor Hills UMC, Colorado Springs; (17) Faith UMC, Sterling; (18) Church and Society with Peace With Justice from Rocky Mountain Conference; (19) Resurrection Fellowship; (20) First Love

Christian Church; (21) Love Outreach Pentecostal Church; (22) Chaplain Sharon French from Larimer County Detention Facility; (23) Sara Choi; (24) Hyon and David Bohnenkamp; (25) Sooja Oh; (26) House of Faith; (27) Good Shepherd Community Church in Pueblo; (28) Rev. Rebekah Simon-Peter; (29) Chapel Hill Church; (30) Rosemary Samson; (31) Mary Trembly; (32) Yolanda Garcia; (33) Cross Connection Church; (34) Immanuel Mission Church; (35) Jean Chase; (36) Edwyne Barney; (37) S.J. Bowman; (38) Dewayne and Robin Stephenson; (39) Carl and Linda Gardner; (40) New Gate Church; (41) Tabitha Bonner; (42) Columbine United Church; (43) Kenneth and Barbara Butcher; (44) Pok Oke; (45) Paradise UMC; (46) Michael and Sue Rayphole; (47) Martha Conant; (48) Joseph Saebi; (49) Laura Nokes Lang; (50) Jonge and Dan Adams; (51) Rev. Olga Jane Hard; (52) Theresa Sande; (53) Larimar County Detention Center; (54) Delores Romero; (55) Marcha Rotty; (56) Good Shepherd UMC; (57) Rev. Hugh Hazel Harris; (58) Flora Luz Movser; (59) Mary and Walter Oswalt; (60) Nick Pacheco; (61) Susan Bianco; (62) Phyllis Blecha; (63) Jack and Kathleen Bloom; (64) Dover UMC; (65) Central UMC, Colorado Springs; (66) Fort Morgan UMC.

Some people donated anonymously, so their names are not included here. Thank you for all your hard work, prayers, support, assistance, and encouragement. God bless you.

INTRODUCTION

Grace Beyond Imagination

This book is possible because of God's grace and the Holy Spirit's leading. In May 2000, after I finished writing *Journey With Jesus*, I was encouraged to write more because God used my story to help others grow spiritually. I asked the Lord what I should write, and He told me to write about dreams.

Since 1997, I have been recording my dreams and interpretations, but I never thought about writing a book. I did not see how a dream book could help others. When I asked God, "Why?" He replied, "My daughter, many of my children ignore their dreams when I try to speak to them. Remind them that I can speak through dreams."

As I was reviewing my journal of dreams, I was greatly encouraged because many things God told me through dreams and interpretations came true. One particular dream I had in January 2000 encouraged me. I had this dream while I was attending The Iliff School of Theology. After I woke up, I asked the Lord for the meaning of the dream. He spoke to me and said that I would receive so many scholarships that I would have to turn some down. I did not think it would be possible, so I forgot about it. Four months later, I was awarded two large scholarships. Because I was involved with prison ministry, I was awarded the Urban ministry scholarship which included a full tuition as a part of the scholarship plus $1,000 each quarter. In addition, I received a Crusade Scholarship from the United Methodist Church, and I received $10,000 each year for the next two years. I had to turn down $7,500 in scholarships because when I received the Crusade Scholarship, one of the requirements was that I would not receive any other United Methodist Scholarship, so others can have the opportunity to receive them. If God did not ask me to write a dream book, I would have forgotten about this dream. I thanked God that what He told me came true.

I selected some of my dreams and included them in my book *Journey With Jesus* in July 2001. Then, in 2005, God told me to make the dream book into a separate book and told me to include Adams County Detention Facility (ACDF) inmates' dreams. I resisted at first because I did not want to spend any more time on a dream book, but the Holy Spirit was persistent.

As I was gathering stories, I learned something new. Many inmates suffered from nightmares because of what they had gone through and where they were. Many were traumatized. I did not understand the extent of their suffering and pain until then. I, too, have suffered from nightmares in the past and was delivered from them with God's power, so I developed a prayer called, "Healing from Nightmares." In our facility, many people who followed the brochures and read the Bible and prayed were delivered from nightmares.

In addition, the Holy Spirit directed me to ask inmates if they had any questions about dreams. Eventually, a section on questions and answers was added with the help of my friend, Michael Goins. Lastly, I added another prayer project, "How to Listen to God's Voice," for those who like to learn how to recognize God's voice through prayer. My prayer is that the Holy Spirit will help you learn how to listen to God and bring healing in your heart and mind.

Drawing "The Power of Prayer" by Bobbie Michel

Part One: Testimonials
ACDF Saints' Reflections and Dreams

1. MY LIFE, MY TOMBSTONE — Alex Flores

About 13 years ago, I had a dream which haunted me, it continued for years until March 15, 2008, to be exact. I have attended the chaplain's worship services every time I have been incarcerated at ACDF. About 10 minutes before the worship services ended, the Chaplain handed us a piece of paper and asked us to write down a dream we had and did not understand or know the meaning of it. This dream came racing back to me, so I wrote it down. She then asked me what I thought it meant.

Years had passed from the date of my dream, and I still did not know the meaning of it. I guess I was procrastinating. In 2007, I was jailed at Denver County jail and ACDF. I was released late November of 2007. I got out thinking I was strong in His Word and firm with the Lord.

A couple of weeks went by sober. I got my old job back, and pretty much everything was good. Just after my release, my wife was incarcerated. I could not wait to see her again. I was set to visit her December 29, 2007, but that visit never happened. She had gotten out without telling anyone. No one knew where she was. Her family would call asking if I knew. As the days went by, I became depressed. I started drinking and using drugs again.

In late January 2008, I finally got a call from my wife. She dropped quite a bomb. She told me our marriage was over. I cried and I told her I loved her and was sure we could work things out. But it was too late. Deep down, I knew she was with someone else and possibly even in love with him. Everything went downhill. I did not care about anything anymore; I fell apart.

After this, I ended up in and out of the emergency room probably around 10 or 11 times. I lost count going from seizures to panic and anxiety attacks. I was fighting on the streets with anyone who even looked at me wrong. I ended up getting stabbed in one of these fights. It was a sign from God. I am now back in ACDF and have been since May 2008. I was only out five months.

It was a blessing from God when I finally came to realize the meaning of the dream. In my dream I was in a cemetery walking toward a grave. I was crying a river of tears and reading a tombstone screaming, "Why? What did you do?" The tombstone had my name and birthdate, but not the date of my death. This dream was so real that when I woke up, I was not only in shock, but in tears as well. My pillow was soaked, and my eyes and cheeks were red from wiping away my tears.

When the Chaplain asked me what I thought it meant, a message came to me in spirit. I knew it came from Father God. We can be like holy shining candles before the Lord, but we are the one who controls our burn. We are gifted with the ability to choose right from wrong in our freedoms. Some of us burn out too quickly, while others just keep on burning until God tells them it's time for them to be with Him.

I thank God for this incarceration, I really do. I was at a down point in life, and coming back here saved me from alcohol, drugs, Satan, possible death, or life imprisonment. My thoughts were thoughts of destruction, hate, bitterness, and even self-hatred.

Father tells us not to love anything or anyone more than Him, and that includes our own family. My marriage was a test from up above, and I guess I loved her more than the Father. That is why He took her from me. My faith was there, but my commitment disappeared. I started to love her more and paid more attention to her, making Him second. How stupid I was, putting the Father second. James Gills, M.D., said in his book, "Just as passion cements the marriage relationship, so it should seal our relationship with God."

We should pray deeply and passionately, making God our highest priority above all other concerns and desires. This passion motivates us to put Him first. Even though I failed the test, God still loves me the same. Intimacy, commitment, and passion for the Father come first in my life now. Through prayer we become closer, and it aligns us with the Father, so pray, pray, pray. This is the key to becoming even more in love with the Father.

With patience, I began to run this race. I'm picking up my cross this time, not leaving it at the door when I leave this place. Every step I take from now on will be for Your loving grace, laughing out loud. Indeed, I will be running this race.

"The Lord is my rock, my fortress and my deliverer; my God is my rock, in whom I take refuge. He is my shield and the horn of my salvation, my stronghold." (Psalm 18:2)

"Hearing that Jesus had silenced the Sadducees, the Pharisees got together. One of them, an expert in the law, tested him with this question: 'Teacher, which is the greatest commandment in the Law?' Jesus replied: 'Love the Lord your God with all your heart and with all your soul and with all your mind.' This is the first and greatest commandment. And the second is like it: *"Love your neighbor as yourself.'* All the Law and the Prophets hang on these two commandments.'" (Matthew 22:34-40) *"Love the Lord your God with all your heart and with all your soul and with all your strength." (Deuteronomy 6:5)*

"Do not love the world or anything in the world. If anyone loves the world, the love of the Father is not in him. For everything in the world--the cravings of sinful man, the lust of his eyes and the boasting of what he has and does--comes not from the Father but from the world. The world and its desires pass away, but the man who does the will of God lives forever." (1 John 2:15-17)

2. NOT TO BE FORGOTTEN — Michael Ernis, written by Joshua O. Cortes

I was born in Antivvorde, Sicily, in 1987. I am now 18 years old. I came to the U.S. in 1989. I am told I was a fine child at the age of three. At the age of two, my biological father divorced my mother. Mr. Bill Ernis, the only father I can remember, then adopted me. I grew closer to Bill than I was to my biological mother.

At the age of four, the worst thing happened to me. I was in the hospital with my dad who was recovering from a heart attack. I was sitting next to him talking and watching TV when my greatest fear became my painful reality. I asked my dad a question but received no answer. So I asked him the question again, and still no answer. I then took it upon myself to look at him to see if he was sleeping, only to find him foaming at the mouth with his eyes rolled back into his head. My mother came into the room and covered my eyes. I remember lights flashing and the monitor alarms going off and then he was gone.

My dad died that night of a fatal heart attack. Witnessing that left me traumatized. For a month and a half afterwards I remained completely speechless and unable to interact with anyone. When I approached seven, I was asked to make an appearance on a show called "Have a Heart" to tell my extremely unfortunate, disturbing, and devastating story of the loss of my father. Shortly after this, I moved out to California where the darkness of suicidal thoughts cast a shadow over my life.

During this time I made 12 different attempts to end my life. I tried everything from hanging myself to slitting my wrists. Needless to say, I struggled with severe depression. I was hospitalized seven times from the age of seven to 17.

As a very young child, I found myself dealing with yet another life-altering tragedy. One afternoon, I was a curious seven-year-old boy walking by a construction site with a desire to display my strength. I picked up a piece of gravel lying near the fence. I tried to throw this football-sized piece of gravel and concrete over the fence. The massive piece of gravel bounced off the fence and landed on the top of my head. It fractured my skull causing internal and external bleeding. I went into cardiac arrest due to a severe loss of blood.

At the hospital, I slipped into a category 5 coma, which lasted for a year and a half. This was a turning point in my life. I remember slipping into a dreamlike state of mind. I found myself on a beach following someone's footsteps, when suddenly that came to a halt. It was at that very moment that I heard the most peaceful sound ever. It was the sound of a man speaking to me from the sky above; he was dressed with the most beautifully colored clouds and rainbows one could imagine. As I continued to look up another man slowly appeared in the sky; that man was none other than Jesus. He began speaking to me, filling my heart with joy, and then I awoke.

Life would never be the same, not only because of my dream, but also because I would have to learn to function again. As an eight and a half year old, I had to learn everything all over again, from potty training to speaking. Yet through it all, I was filled with a genuine desire to know this man they call Jesus, whom I felt I owed my life to. Come to find out, I always had.

The doctor had officially diagnosed me with an extremely rare form of internal brain damage known as dementia (a severe short

-term memory loss.) The diagnosis was that by the time I reached the age of 30, I wouldn't have any memory past a three-hour span. I wouldn't be able to remember my childhood, my first kiss, my first love, my first ball game, or even my first child. According to them, I wouldn't even remember writing this paper or sharing my testimony with you.

I beg to differ, however, now that I've taken time to get to know that kind man who appeared in my dream, I've come to know some things that those doctors must not have known; and that is that all things are possible through our Father in heaven.

In fact, it was Jesus himself, who, in *Matthew 8:15-16*, touched the hand of Peter's mother-in-law and made the fever leave her body. He drove the evil spirits out of people controlled by demons with a mere word, healing all who were sick. That's not to mention all the hundreds of other miracles that have been performed by Jesus Christ, including waking me up out of my coma, and even providing me with the capability of speaking and writing this testimony.

If there is one thing I remember best, however, it is what the prophet Isaiah said in chapter *53:4, "Surely he took up our infirmities and carried our sorrows, yet we considered him stricken by God, smitten by him, and afflicted."* Now I do not know about you, but to me that says it all. I am just not willing to forget.

3. I THANK JESUS FOR THIS MOMENT — Monica Valdez

I was in a very bad situation, and I knew my boys did not deserve to witness my madness. Desperately, I called my mom and asked her to please pick up the boys. I knew I was going back to my old ways. That day police showed up at my door because of a domestic situation, and the father of my youngest son was taken from me.

The police officer went through my purse and found some marijuana. He cuffed me and dragged me to his car. I was begging him not to take me. My son, Jacob, was asleep and my oldest son, Julian, was in school. The officer told me that Social Services would pick up my children. I started to scream and cry. I was begging him not to take my children and me away. As the officer put me in the back of the police car, my mother pulled into the driveway. She had driven from San Diego, California, to Colorado. God made all these things possible. He was there the whole time, I just did not know it. My mom took my boys to San Diego with her.

I was released from ACDF, and was involved in a serious accident one month later. In June 2004, a friend of mine passed away because of a drug overdose. She was young with a husband and two beautiful children. I could feel a very strong presence of confusion, sadness and loss in their house. Even then I could see evil all over and felt guilt. December 24, 2004, was my friend's daughter's birthday, and her father was a mess. He was so into his own madness and getting high that he was being consumed by drugs and the devil. That day my life changed forever.

It was early, and I was on my way to the house to make a birthday breakfast for my friend's daughter, her friends, and her young brother. A woman was cut off by a drunk driver on the only part of the highway without a guardrail. The woman lost control of her vehicle, crossed over into oncoming traffic at 65 miles an hour, and she hit my vehicle head on. I had just picked up two kids. Thank God nothing happened to them. I had put them in their seat belts and made sure they were buckled right.

I do not remember anything, but the kids told me later what happened. They said that I saw the lady coming toward us from the other side. I could not avoid her. She plowed right into us. I was going 60 miles per hour on impact. She hit us so hard the engine blew 140 feet out the side of the van. The boys told me that after she hit us, I tried to get to them to make sure they were okay, but I could not move. I was pinned, so I cried and passed out.

Three months later I woke up from a coma at Denver Health Hospital. All I could remember was a dream I had of a man walking with me. At first, I was alone in a crazy carnival. As I was walking from the carnival, all of a sudden I was in a beautiful, peaceful garden. A man was walking by my side, and I was not afraid. He told me that I was going to be okay.

When I woke up, I still did not know where I was. I could not walk. Both my legs were broken, and my jaw and back were hurt. I had almost bled to death. My leg had been ninety percent severed and was hanging by the bone. That day I should have died. The paramedics and police were amazed that I was still alive and that the children were not injured. They tried to save my leg. Since no one could give consent to amputate, they left it the way it was, but it was useless.

I spent the next couple of months in the critical-care unit. I was told it would be better to amputate, but I refused. Even then I did not listen to the Lord or thank Him for not letting my soul burn in Hell. I was blessed, and I did not realize how much the Lord was with me. I did not know that through this I would come to the Lord and He would start building me up with His love through my appreciation for not letting me die.

When I was released from the hospital, my friend, the father of the two children, was supposed to pick me up. I turned on the news only to see him busted in a big raid in Thornton. I was picked up from the hospital by some other friends. Once I left the hospital, I went back to my old ways – the only ways that I knew. I had given up. I had lost whatever faith and love I had had for God and myself.

The house was a wreck. The person taking care of the place had been selling everything, and I was in a wheelchair. Many bad things happened in that house. I was using and selling drugs. One day a guy showed up with duct tape and a baseball bat to rob me. I was in my wheelchair, and I could see by the coldness of his eyes that he was ready to do something very bad. I might not live and neither money nor drugs will ever be worth my life. I talked him out of hurting me. He went to look for my money and drugs and left me by myself.

I tried to walk and fell out the door. The neighbor called the police. The guy was caught two days later. He shot somebody two blocks from my house in a home invasion, and then got into a police chase. I think he was coming back to kill me. He eventually received 72 years for his crime.

Now I know that I was on the road to death, not just of the body, but of the soul. I was depressed. I was suicidal and homicidal. I was stealing cars while I was on crutches. I wanted to die. I was angry that I would never be the same physically, but what good would it be if my soul died as well? Police chases, dope, and guns were my thing. My left leg was rotting, and I did not care.

After the accident, I did not realize that if all I lost was my leg I should be grateful and thank the Lord. I would walk again with my children and the Lord. All these things, even ending up in jail, saved my life.

I was brought back to ACDF in July 2006. Ending up in Adams County jail, the coma, and the loss of my leg, and not my life, were blessings. When I arrived here, I was dying of infection in my leg, and I did not care. I did not see how God had worked everything the way He did, so I would be able to know His love and faith within me. If God had not been taking care of me, I would have lost my life, my children, and my soul for all eternity.

I began to cry and pray to the Lord. For the first time, I started to feel God's love and the Holy Spirit. In those days, I occasionally prayed with the chaplain and with some other inmates in the pod. I asked the Lord to help me. He lets me know that if I ever wanted to walk with my children or take care of them, I would have to have my leg amputated. I finally accepted the fact that I needed to do it. I asked the doctors in the infirmary and at Denver Health Hospital to go ahead and do it.

I felt the Holy Spirit more than any other time in my life the night before my surgery. I was reading a letter from my son. As I sat there, I felt a beautiful presence of love and power come from behind me. The girl sitting next to me looked at me and said, "Did you feel that?"

I prayed that night and cried. I told God, "I can get through this only with You by my side." Then I understood all the ways His love had saved me. I was scared, but I knew that I had to accept what was happening and live for my children, my faith, and believe in what the Lord was doing.

On the morning of the operation, September 6, 2006, I woke up and went to see the magazines that had been brought for me. The first one I looked at was about prostheseses and not giving up no matter what. God was letting me know He was with me. Not even 15 minutes later, my name was called, and I was on my way to the hospital. "Mrs. Walker" is the deputy who was with me and saw how I was crying on the operating table. She prayed with me and cried with me. But I was not afraid. I knew that everything has a purpose. She spoke to me about my boys and told me that I had to be strong. She told me that I was making the right choice and to think about my boys. That's what gave me strength.

Later, I was so very upset and depressed that I was brought down to the infirmary. I had never before felt such conflict. I felt a presence of evil spirits around me and was filled with fear. I saw the demons that had been sent to destroy my faith. I even questioned my own sanity. The doctors told me it was all in my head or a reaction to the pills (meds). I knew the only doctor that could help me was the Lord.

I thought it was a curse to see the actual spiritual battle and how real it is. The devil tempted me to the point of doubting my sanity and brought to my attention how weak my faith was. I was very vulnerable through all those attacks. The enemy was whispering that I could not be forgiven. He made me feel guilty that my children were with my mother and not with me. I was falling into his trap, but the Lord has perfect timing.

I knew what was wrong with me, and I also knew what I needed. My faith and love of the Father must be stronger than anything else. He sent a worker of His harvest to help me. Every time I was being attacked and fear was consuming me, the Chaplain showed up and prayed with me or talked to me about how the spiritual attacks are so real. Her books and testimony of her life, and the testimonies of the Maximum Saints books written by the incarcerated are a last chance for many.

God has been with me this whole time. I have been at the right place at all times. I just have to thank Jesus and praise Him for His sacrifice. He gave His life for this world. I just did not know it. My kids might have been with me the day of the wreck. Now I realize all that happened the way it has was the work of the Lord: my mom picking up my boys, my accident, ending up in Adams County, the coma, and the loss of my leg and not my life. These events helped me to humble myself and put my faith in the Lord. I now understand what the spiritual battle is: fight to the death against the flesh and desires of this world. I am writing my testimony to help others. I feel the Holy Spirit working in me as I write this, and this gives me hope.

John 9:1 helps me to understand how wonderful God is. When the disciples saw a blind man, they asked who sinned: his parents or the man who had been born blind. Jesus replied, "Neither this man nor his parents sinned, but this happened so that the work of God might be displayed in his life."

I truly feel that God spoke to me through that scripture. Even though I received three years in community corrections and am waiting for a bed, I thank God for opening my eyes to the truth. I will never be the same. I thank Jesus for this moment.

4. KEEP STRIVING UPWARDS — Leilani Sharp

In my dream, I was in a place like a stadium. I looked down and saw nothing but bright fire, then I looked up and saw people. Some were already seated, and some were still climbing upward. Somehow I knew that if I walked down the stairs, I would be walking the path to hell. If I walked up the stairs, it was to be with the Lord. I felt tired and knew it would be easier to just walk down the stairs, but that's not what I wanted. I wanted to be with Jesus and all the others that were sitting down. They looked as if they were waiting for something. They also looked as if they did not mind, because whatever they were waiting for was worth the wait.

I started to climb upwards, but there were obstacles in my way. It was either running into someone from the past that stopped me or just not knowing which way to go. I was desperate to get around those obstacles because I knew that when I reached the top I would get the most amazing reward to be with Jesus.

I grew up as a Christian, but I fell away and walked down the wrong path. I even got to the point where I denied that He even existed. I thought my life was better off without Him. It took me years to realize that my life was not better off no matter what I did. I always felt like there was something missing. I felt lonely no matter how many people I had around me. I got tired of crying myself to sleep every night, but I did not know what to do.

I eventually got arrested again and was brought to Adams County Jail. It was tough. I thought it was the worst thing that could be happening in my life at that time. I had to withdraw from drugs. Now I realize it was the best thing because it brought me back to the Lord. I found people to do Bible study with every day. For once in about six years, I do not have that empty, lonely feeling in my heart. I'm clean and sober. I even got to see my daughter. Now that I have the Lord back in my life, I need to "keep striving upwards" and not fall back to taking the easy way again. I know where the easy path leads: down.

5. WHAT CAN I DO TO MAKE YOU SMILE? — Sherry Hinton

I was having bad, bad dreams. Some were crack dreams, some were just nightmares of all sorts. Sometimes I would be getting high. Other times I would have the crack in my hand or the pipe in my mouth. It always turns out that they were just dreams. The nightmare was intense. I was being chased through alleys, up and down streets, buying and selling crack.

God saved me by putting me in jail. He let me know the reason for my bad dreams and nightmares was the result of my sin. He said I could, and would, be able to get rid of my sins by being obedient to His Word and keeping His commandments. Once I prayed and began doing what He said, then, and only then, did He heal me.

Now I can sleep without smoking crack in my dreams. Now I can sleep without running up and down alleys. Now I am healed and delivered. I am now thanking God for sending His Son, Jesus, who died for me.

For everyone who reads this, learn to be obedient to the words of the Lord. Learn to keep His commandments. It works. I was healed through reading the Bible, praising the Lord, praying, being obedient to the Word, and forgiving others.

When Noah built the Ark, God looked down and smiled because he was obedient. I asked God, "What can I do to make You smile?" The answer was, "If you love Me, you will obey My commandments." When you pray, ask the Lord what you can do to make Him smile. Our Creator likes to smile, too, when He looks down on us. I pray for you all. God bless.

6. I AM THANKFUL TO KNOW HIM — Wendi Harmon

When I was 13, my parents were getting a divorce, and I felt I was the one getting a divorce. My mother beat us. My sister, brother, and my Dad just left. I did not know who God or Jesus was at the time.

When I turned 15 years old, I was a very bad girl. I was doing things that caused my parents and friends to be very ashamed of me. I was wearing black and was into black magic. All the things that I was doing were mean things to people. I did not believe in the Lord because I was hurt as a child. I asked, "Why would God let my parents divorce? Why does my mother beat me all the time?"

On September 17, 1992, I was coming home from my friend's house. We were playing around, and she bumped me off the curb. As I turned around to get off the street, a van going 45 miles an hour hit me. I flew 20 feet in the air. All I remember was that I heard the Flight for Life saying, "We are losing her." I slipped into a coma for three weeks.

I remember the dream that I had in my coma. I was standing on a cliff somewhere. It was very dark and very hot. I looked down and saw bugs clawing all over me and eating my flesh. I felt my body melting and I could hear people screaming for help. I said, "Where am I?" Then I can remember seeing clouds, flowers, rainbows, things that are colorful. I heard a voice, "Will you be with me?" I said, "Yes." That was the Lord speaking to me so that I would change my life. I would burn in hell if I did not choose the Lord.

When I finally woke up, my dad, my family and other people I did not know were there. I had suffered a massive head injury. I had bleeding in three parts of my brain and my hip and wrist were both broken. I was in 7th grade when this happened. I had to start all over, walking and talking again. Two years later, I walked out of Children's Hospital on July 7, 1994.

When I went back home, my mother was a different person. My old room was painted wonderful colors instead of black. I had a brand new Bible sitting on my table, and my Mom said, "Welcome home, my miracle child."

On October 21, 1995, while going through rehab, I met a man I would marry. We were together for about 10 months and got married. In 1997, our first son was born. I had been told I was not ever going to have a child because I was hit by a car. My son is 11 years old now. I know the Lord gave me this marriage and a son. I've been married to the same guy – happily married. We lost a daughter in 2006. She was two years old when she passed away, but I know God and Jesus are with her.

I've been in jail a lot over the years, and I guess I've never learned to stay out of the system. I'm in here for something that happened last year. My husband did something very wrong in our marriage. I hurt him and he was taken to the hospital. I was arrested. I had also hurt myself. I had four stitches in my wrist when I went to jail. I thought to myself, "Why am I here? My husband should be here because he hurt me more than anything in this world." I thought of dying. I also thought that it's time to grow with the Lord.

On June 3, 2008, Pod 5 had a group prayer. A Christian brother and Chaplain came to pray with us. That day I asked the Lord for forgiveness, and I repented of my sins from what I had done as a child as well as through my life, years of shame, guilt, hurt, and anger. Then the following Sunday, I went to the chaplain's worship service, and I was baptized. That night I was not feeling well, so I was sent to medical because I was having disturbing thoughts. All week I've been having very bad dreams.

God had been showing me in my heart that life is wonderful. However, my dreams have been very scary, and I cry because they are bad. One dream that I can tell you is that I died. I was so mangled that no one could identify me, so they just threw my body away. In reality, I could have been dead many times, but God kept me alive. When I was in medical, the Chaplain came and said that dreams may represent spiritual warfare going on in my life. She told me to stay strong with the Lord through reading the Bible and through prayer.

I read my Bible almost every day. I like the book of *Malachi* and *Ephesians 1:4-9: "For he chose us in him before the creation of the world to be holy and blameless in his sight. In love he predestined us to be adopted as his sons through Jesus Christ, in accordance with his pleasure and will--to the praise of his glorious grace, which he has freely given us in the One he loves. In him we have redemption through his blood, the forgiveness of sins, in accordance with the riches of God's grace that he lavished on us with all wisdom and understanding. And he made known to us the mystery of his will according to his good pleasure, which he purposed in Christ."*

I've been down that broken road – Department of Corrections (DOC) – pretty much all of my life. I'm spending more time in ACDF than with my family. I'm almost done, and I can go home to be with my family and tell my son and my husband about how I have become more in love with the Lord. Amen!

The Lord does have a purpose for me. I could have died 16 years ago from my car wreck, and many times I've come close to overdosing on drugs or having thoughts of suicide, but God saved me. Some of these ladies here at ACDF opened my eyes. I am here for a reason and I pray that God will reveal it to me.

7. THE LORD HAS TRANSFORMED MY LIFE — Lonnie Jovan Griego

When I got to Adams County Jail in 2008, they placed me in B Module in the maximum pod. I ran into an old friend, Santos, who used to do all kinds of sinning with me on the street. He told me he had given his life to Christ. The thought had crossed my mind in Intake about changing my life, but I had not acted on it. Now, my friend was right here telling me how this new life has given him peace and made him a new man, and how Christ has touched him.

Something was tugging at me, and I knew that's what I wanted. Then we flushed the old me down the toilet! Santos was telling me about this guy named Jon (Jonathan Willis), who helped him grow in Christ and how he was a really good dude who loved the Lord. He wanted me to meet him. Jon just so happened to be upstairs asleep at the time. All through lockdown I was excited about making this change and meeting this guy who helped my boy. The door popped open, and I looked out and saw Santos standing upstairs by the corner cell talking to someone who was in the cell. He waved for me to come upstairs, so I headed up there. I was about 10 feet away, and low and behold, this 6-foot, blond-haired, blue-eyed white guy stepped out of the cell. I'm thinking, "You've got to be kidding me." Santos did most of the talking. Then Jonathan spoke directly to me saying something like, "I commend you for what you did by getting rid of the old you and stepping out in faith. This walk isn't gonna be easy, but as long as you put Christ first in everything you do, He will make a way." Then he hit me with some Scriptures to read.

Santos left the next morning, so the only person I knew in the pod was Jonathan. Imagine that! He opened his heart to me providing me with everything I needed, because I had missed commissary day. He was always saying, "Do not worry about it," with a big smile, never expecting anything back.

Being a "fetus in Christ," I had a thousand questions. Every time I'd shoot them at Jonathan, he'd shoot back with Scriptures and what the Bible says. I admired that so much. That's how I knew he was authentic. One time my grandfather told me that that's how you know if a preacher is real or not: if what he says can be cross-referenced (backed up) by Scriptures in the Bible!

From then on, I fellowshipped with Jonathan every day in the Word of God, in prayer, fasting, discussing all types of life situations, family, relationships and everything else you can think of! We formed a three-cord braid *(Ecclesiastes 4:12):* Jonathan Willis, Adam Ramirez and myself. I thank the Lord for Jonathan Willis. I do not know where I'd be without him.

One day I had a revelation through a dream which has helped me understand my spiritual condition. In the dream, the old sinful, disrespectful person I used to be, was in a restaurant, and I was cussing and acting out, humiliating people – the waiter and other customers. As I was walking out, something or someone grabbed my hand and placed something over my head. I was in complete darkness and fear came over me. I was terrified. I did not know where we were going. When the cover was taken off my head, we were in an empty white room. My focus was blurry, but I could see a childlike figure on the ground that was deformed, crippled and hurting. For some reason, I knew I had hurt this child. I felt remorse and a great sorrow. I began to cry and apologize. When my eyes began to focus, I could see his face. It was my face as a grown man on a child's body. When I woke up, I was feeling the same sorrow as in the dream. I got on my knees and asked God to forgive me.

This is my interpretation of the dream. The Lord was showing me how all the sinful things I used to do have hurt and brought pain upon myself. It was through my street life and addiction to drugs that I had hurt this child of God. This dream reminds me of the story of Paul on his way to Damascus when Jesus knocked him off of the horse and blinded him, asking him, *"Why do you persecute me?" (Acts 9:1-6)* Paul had a reputation for hurting children of God. That's why he was on his way to Damascus in the first place. Jesus blinded him, then sent a disciple to him so he could see again and be filled with the Holy Spirit. Not only were his outward eyes open so he could see, but his spiritual eyes were opened as well so he could see the things of God.

After I lost everything and almost lost my life to prison, I made the decision that I cannot do it on my own. I gave my all to Christ, and through God's grace and mercy, He has accepted me and changed my life around. Through obedience to the Word of God, prayer and fasting, the Lord has transformed my life. I'm happy and excited to say He is not finished with me yet!

8. I SERVE THE LORD — Timothy Garcia

I am 31 years old and grew up in the East Denver projects. My mom was a single mother who did the best that she could. I was always getting into fights with other kids. When I was about eight or nine years old, my mom tried putting me into private Christian schools: Annunciation, Riverview Christian Academy, now called Faith Christian Academy, and Loyola Christian Academy. I got thrown out of all these schools within one year.

By the time I was 14 years old, I was already drinking beer. I was carrying a gun and committing bad crimes that kept getting worse. I would take my gun to school, and even take it to class. One time, my gun fell on the floor during class. I picked it up and walked out, but nobody told on me. The only reason I went to school was to have fun and chill.

As time went on, I kept getting into trouble. By the time I was 16, I was drinking beer every day. When I was 19 years old, I was sentenced to one year in Denver County Jail. When I got out of jail, I still struggled with my homies. Every morning, I would drink a 40 ounce Old English and then go to school. I was always getting into trouble.

In 2000, I started playing with a Ouija Board. I used it to talk to demons, and I tried to summon Satan so I could talk to him. I did magic. I also summoned people's family that had died. It would let me contact any person that had died and was with Satan in hell. The Ouija Board would let me do supernatural things. Eventually, I started praying to Satan and asked him to fill me with legions of demons.

One day I knew Satan really wanted me, so I put the Ouija Board away and left the apartment. As I was walking to the liquor store, I saw a black backpack on the ground. It was open, and there were books scattered all over the sidewalk. I picked up one of the books. It had a black cover, and I turned the book over to see the title on the cover. It had the satanic pentagram star on it. The book was filled with satanic spells. It even had a spell of how to have somebody killed by putting a curse on them. I was excited at the time because I knew the book was there for me.

I started praying to Satan, and I ended up catching a case and getting three years in prison. Even though I was in prison, I kept praying to Satan. I would make an Ouija Board out of notebook paper and it was just like a real Ouija Board. I had also experienced Satan's power through gambling. I had been winning a lot gambling in prison. I would use the Ouija Board to gamble and to pick football through the Ouija Board and win. Satan was telling me that I could go to Las Vegas and win a lot of money. I learned what Satan promised was a lie.

Since 2002, I've been in and out of prison a lot. This case that I'm facing can send me back to prison. This will be the fifth time, but I have great news! I have finally accepted Jesus Christ as my Lord and Savior. I've been a born again Christian since March 16, 2008.

When I first arrived at ACDF, I was suicidal and just fed up with the world. Then I started to read the Maximum Saints books and the stories in the books showed me that there were other guys going through the same thing that I was. It made me want to give my heart to the Lord and to surrender to the Lord. The Lord helped and strengthened my spirit through the Maximum Saints books. Now I've been baptized and have given my life to the Lord, which I had never done until now. My heart is now content and filled with joy, and I give all the glory to God. It also feels great to know I am going to heaven.

My turning point came because worshiping Satan was destroying my life. Satan lied to me, promising me supernatural power, a lot of money, and women. I never had any peace in my heart or in my mind. Also, I realized that if I kept serving the devil, I would either end up dead or doing a life sentence in prison. I was on suicide watch and I did not want to live any more. I knew Satan was destroying me.

I had a dream when I was 11 years old that a demon-possessed man was trying to get me and my mother in our apartment. We were running from him all around our apartment. My mother who was a Christian was trying to protect and help me. She is now very happy that I've become a Christian.

When I was 25 years old, I had a dream that a giant black spider was trying to get me. The spider had gold armor. It was chasing me, but it could not catch me. A guy I used to hang out with at that time was a Satanist who would interpret my dreams for me. He would speak a satanic language and would tell me what position I was going to have in Satan's kingdom. He would get possessed by a demon after we were done drinking alcohol and doing drugs, and it scared me.

I believe the devil was torturing me in my dreams and I did not know how to fight back then. But now that I'm a born again Christian, I can be strong, and God is helping me get through this. I have repented of the sins that I've committed and gave my life to be a living sacrifice to the Lord. Spiritual battles continue, and I continue to fight. I put on the full armor of God every day. It's spiritual warfare every day, all day long. Demons are constantly attacking me, and I bind them all day in the blood of Jesus. I know Satan really wanted me. He lied to me and deceived me. He tried to destroy me, and he's still trying. Whenever I really get attacked by demons, I get on my knees and pray.

I read the Bible and Christian books all day. The more I pray, the better my day. I have to pray all day. I give Jesus Christ and the Father all the glory. I cannot succeed in life without the Lord. I should be dead right now, but the Lord wants me alive so I can bring people to Him. Once I am free again, knowing I have the Holy Spirit in me, I will have on the full armor of God and be ready for Satan's temptations and the spiritual war. *"Put on the full armor of God so that you can take your stand against the devil's schemes." (Ephesians 6:11)*

The Lord is my best friend. I now have a personal relationship with the Lord. The Lord is real, and if you are a person who has not asked Him into your heart, now is the time. Ask the Lord to forgive you for all your sins and fill you with the Holy Spirit. Fear the Lord, pray for mercy, and repent. Believe me, you never want to feel the Lord's wrath.

If you are a Satan worshipper, you are being selfish and destructive. Ask God for forgiveness and you will find peace. He will forgive you no matter what you've done. *"If we confess our sins, he is faithful and just and will forgive us our sins and purify us from all unrighteousness." (1 John 1:9)*

Give your life to the Lord, so you can help others. I serve the Lord, and I am trying to help others. The Lord is giving me a great inner peace. I give Him all the glory and all the praise every day.

9. JESUS, I GIVE YOU THE GLORY — Monica Valdez

When I was 20 years old, I had this dream. At the time, I lived in South Dakota and California with a bunch of my friends. We were all looking for something (God). One day I woke up from a dream, and I never forgot what it was telling me about the days to come. There was a river and a mountain, and I was a warrior in the last days. I took my family outside by a river and up a mountain to hide, so they would be safe since everything was chaos.

I was fighting the evil of the world. I was running and saw an old church. I ran inside to see if anyone was left, so I could get them somewhere safe. When I was inside there was a woman running up and down the aisle of the church. She was wearing a summer dress, had lots of make up and big hair, holding two baskets. She was in such a panic. She was screaming for money as if that would save her.

On one side of the pews was a man and on the other side were four elderly people. They were calm, praying and not concerned about the crazy lady or the war. They asked me if I would sit down with them. They were so peaceful that even as the fighting was going on, they were not afraid.

Then I heard a man weeping on the other side of the pews. As I walked over there, I realized the man crying was my father. He had a picture of a little girl in his hand. He was so sad because he had lost his daughter. He said, "My daughter, my daughter. She is gone." I looked at my father and replied, "Dad, I am not lost. I'm here. Please don't cry. Look at me." He would not, but asked me for a Bible because he needed to pray. His daughter was lost and he could not find her.

So, I looked around for a Bible but there were none. I had no time. I needed to keep fighting the evil army of the devil. We were at war. The children of God against the children of the devil. I ran out of the church. All of a sudden, I could see some kind of bombs being set to destroy the world, and I woke up.

I was really moved by this dream and I could not stop

thinking about it. I went to work that day. It was a beautiful day. I walked from 25th and Broadway to 1stand started making my calls, as I was a telemarketer. At noon I went out for a smoke. I sat down, and someone had left a Bible on the bench. I will never forget that day or how God had been calling me. I'm realizing more and more how much God has been waiting for me to stop, listen and learn. Much wisdom comes with great sorrow and with knowledge, much grief.

Another dream that scared me was about being chased by demons. I had this dream while here in Adams County Jail in January 2008. Some demons were big, some were like regular people, and others were like the night of the living dead. I was in one of these dreams in a haze. I was in a cemetery where these traitors had a stack of bodies. The demons would try to catch me so they could put me in one of the holes; each one was already filled with about 30 heads. They were shipping people off to get rid of them like animals. They kept trying to catch me, but I would jump like I was on a bungee cord; bouncing around, so they still could not catch me.

I was always looking for answers. The devil had made me a slave for 15 years and I was the living dead. I was looking but could not see, and now I am ready to tell everyone that God is real. It is a matter of life and death to those who believe and to the ones who don't. God, our Father, Jesus Christ, and the Holy Spirit are the only things that matter in this world. So don't become corrupt and controlled by the puppet master, the devil.

I am just a baby in my faith and Christ, but the more I read Maximum Saints books and my Bible, the better I understand. I do not preach, yet, but I have received my answer. I asked God to please tell me what to do. He said, "Change your ways. Time is running out. Save yourself and save as many as you can."

My dreams scare me sometimes because I know the spiritual world is real. I see angels in my room, as well as in my dreams. They are the most beautiful amazing things I've ever seen. God is real. Jesus is real. Death is real and so is life. God has opened my eyes and has even sent me guardian angels. I did not plan this, God did. I will never be the same. This has changed me to believe in the Lord. As I am writing this, there is an angel that stays over me. I can see it so clearly. They are not being shy with me. I wish other people could see what I'm seeing. There is a big angel holding the hand of a smaller one. I asked him if I could see them up close, and they were okay with it.

What a blessing for me to see them. I am grateful for this gift, though I question, "Why me?" I know it's because God has made it possible for me to be used as a worker in the harvest and a sister to all God's children. He is going to open a lot of doors. He already has. This moment is what I've lived for. The Lord has prepared me for this so I could witness such an amazing thing and tell people about it. I really feel and know that many people will be saved by my testimony.

There is a heaven and hell. The devil and his crew are nothing close to God's love; they live in darkness. They hide and attack. They want to attack as much of the world as possible. They work overtime to destroy as many as possible. Please save your soul, your families, strangers, friends, and everybody else who you come in contact with. Live for today and save as many as you can. Just tell them about Jesus and pray that every soul will listen and not be held captive prisoners to an eternal torture and death with no hope. I can feel the sorrow and the grief of others and myself at times. Deep in my heart I know the Lord takes away all fear and I am His.

Today is June 10, 2008. It's been three weeks since my whole life changed. Some do not believe, some do. Some think I am crazy, some think it's cool. At first, all I would see was angels. Not only that, God has opened my eyes to see angels fighting with demons in a battle for my soul right in front of my eyes. I get scared at times thinking they might take my soul. I pray, "Lord, please show me what to do. Change me. I am still so new to your love." I pick up the Bible and read the Word. "Please, I need you Lord. Take the enemy away from me."

I am so grateful to be chosen to witness such a spiritual blessing in my life. I will tell everyone I can talk to and speak of what it means to be a witness of the power of the Lord. He has sent his angels to protect me when I am being attacked. I am no longer scared.

I'm starting to understand what my calling is more and more each day. I see these beautiful creations sent not to just some people, but to all. I am just barely realizing how long the Lord has been waiting patiently for me and how much time I wasted. "Father, forgive me. I know you have been there and you still chose to wait. I thank you, Father. Thank you. Lord, you have called me. I will do anything you ask of me. I'm trying to tame the tongue that speaks foul language or deceit." I now know how real all this is, and how I will be used in this spiritual warfare to see angels as well as demons.

I always felt like I did not deserve anything, and I've been so tired of believing in a hopeless life, but I do not feel that way anymore. "God, please do not let me lose my last chance to show my family that I'm changing my life. Jesus, I give you the glory. You gave me the grace. I am nothing without you. Can you see it in my face?"

10. SPIRITS OF TORMENT — Christian "Nicole" Sandoval

In a dream, I was helping clean the house of a white woman, a Chinese man and four children. Three of the children were not hers, and the last one was from an affair. The woman held unforgiveness, resentment, jealousy, hurt, pride, disappointment, rebellion, and a feeling of unworthiness. I laid hands on her and prayed the blood of Jesus would wash over her.

Legions of demons were in this household. I started to do battle. The demons came four and five deep to the front door of the house. I'd answer the door and send them away in Jesus' name. They would look at me with hate-filled eyes. I'd walked up to a window and closed and locked it saying, "Keep the windows closed." All the while, the demons kept trying to get inside where the man and wife were arguing. I was trying to keep the peace. I felt empowered by the Holy Spirit the entire dream.

The demons were sneaking in through the windows. Someone kept opening up the windows in the house. I remembered the Scripture: *"Have no fear of sudden disaster or of the ruin that overtakes the wicked." (Proverbs 3:25)* On two occasions I was pleading that the blood of Jesus would come over the family, and casting demons out by laying of hands on the woman and protecting her by the blood of Jesus. Also, I occasionally was walking from room to room, casting demons out in Jesus' mighty name. There were so many!

On the last occasion, I felt them behind me as I was trying to comfort the husband and wife. I turned around and saw three demons that kept coming in and tormenting the family. I started to cast them out in the name of Jesus. They got pushed back for a minute but came back at me with laughing faces. I started asking God to cover me with the blood of Jesus to protect me. I then started to praise God's name, lifting up my hands. I felt frustrated because they wouldn't go.

Then all of a sudden my son was by my side and joined in the fight. We both started to push the evil forces back as a team, casting out and immobilizing them in the mighty name of our Savior Jesus, by the blood of Jesus and with God's praises and lifting up Jesus' name. We were successful in overcoming them and shouted hallelujah, then I woke up.

This dream is about my household. The woman is myself, the Chinese man is J and the children refer to relationships. J kept opening the windows and letting demons in the house. I've been fighting for our relationship to be healed. I've tried to walk away. I've been fasting and praying. I feel frustrated over this. I'm the woman holding onto unforgiveness, rebellion, resentment, feelings of unworthiness, rejection, and jealousy. J had an affair while I've been sitting here at ACDF.

I'm also holding on to our relationship out of compassion and sincere love for the man. He has been sneaking around, using drugs, lying to himself and trying to lie to me, which is like him, opening the windows letting in demons.

Through this dream, I felt like God was trying to tell me I could not fight this battle alone. I need another believer to pray for deliverance. God was revealing my spiritual condition and that was an answer to prayer on why it continues to torment me; why I'm not able to let go. God has also shown me the way out for us. Tools for spiritual warfare include: 1) Faith 2) A clean heart 3) The Holy Spirit 4) The blood of Jesus 5) The name of Jesus 6) Fellowship 7) Prayer 8) Praying together 9) Perseverance 10) Compassion 11) Knowledge and 12) Courage.

"So, Jesus called them and spoke to them in parables: 'How can Satan drive out Satan? If a kingdom is divided against itself, that kingdom cannot stand. If a house is divided against itself, that house cannot stand. And if Satan opposes himself and is divided, he cannot stand; his end has come. In fact, no one can enter a strong man's

house and carry off his possessions unless he first ties up the strong man. Then he can rob his house.'" (Mark 3:23-27) "Calling the Twelve to him, he sent them out two by two and gave them authority over evil spirits." (Mark 6:7)

11. IF YOU ASK, YOU SHALL RECEIVE — Dianne Meier

I had three babies to raise on my own. I continued using cocaine off and on. Then, I was introduced to meth. At first I just used it on weekends, but then I liked the way it made me feel. It gave me energy and I lost weight. For some reason, I actually started liking myself, so I began using it daily. Before I knew it, I was so wrapped up in the twisted world of meth that I lost my children and was locked up.

In jail, I realized I had no one who really cared about me. No one liked me. No one! Not one of the people I called my friend would help me. No one visited me, not even my own family. They were never there for me before, so I did not expect them to be there for me now.

After being jailed several times and later having three possession charges, I found myself here at Adams County where I met two wonderful ladies, Anna and Angela. They both have helped me to see that our lives can change because Jesus died for our sins. "If only you will open your mind and your heart," they said, "You will soon see that Jesus will forgive you and help you."

I started reading the Bible and praying for the first time in my life. Angela told me I needed to sit alone and talk to the Lord. Ask Him to show me my sins and to show me what I needed to do. "If you ask, you will see," she said. "Do not be afraid because God will never give you more than you can handle."

So I did. That night the Lord and I had a long talk. I asked Him for a lot of things. I also asked Him to forgive me. I asked the Lord to show me what to do about my children! I had a parent's rights hearing in just a few days. I was so scared that I would lose my rights since I was a meth user. That evening, in my dreams, the Lord showed me what to do. I dreamt my daughter was sitting on my lap, and I was asking her how she would feel about being adopted by Ted and Gail. She smiled at me and said, "Mommy, its okay if it has to be that way right now, but you're still my mommy, and I will always get to see you." I told her I loved her, and she gave me a big hug and said she loved me, too. Then I woke up and almost started crying when I realized it was a dream and my daughters weren't really on my lap. The Lord showed me what I needed to do in a dream! I truly believed then and opened my mind and soul to the Lord.

12. I FEEL GOD LIVES IN MY HEART — Meseret Atanaw Wassie

I am 29 years old and a native of Sudan, Africa. I have been here in America since 1990. This is my testimony about what Christ Jesus has done for me since I have been here in ACDF. I've been on my own since I was 14. I never had a close family, and have done anything and everything on the street. My way never got me anywhere but prison and jail.

Before I found God, I used to say bad things about God. I was brought here for something I did not do. I started thinking about why I was here, and I asked God to help me with this. God showed me that I was mean. He showed me what mean and hateful things I have said and done to my wife and other people. I started to cry and I asked God to forgive me for what I have done. I also asked Him to help me get rid of my anger.

When I received Jesus Christ into my heart, things started to get harder every day. I got baptized on May 8, 2008, and after that, my walk was difficult. My family turned their back on me and my wife left me, but that was the Lord's plan for me.

As time went by, I realized that I had lost everything. God told me to let my wife go, to leave it to Him and to have faith in Him. God meant it for good! As Christians, we believe that God is able to make all things work for our good the way the Bible says. God takes whatever happens to us and makes the best of it, sort of a secondhand blessing. But God isn't on the defensive. He isn't limited to making the best out of a bad situation. God takes the initiative! We need to remind ourselves of that every so often. I realize now that through struggle and pain, unless someone stands up to make a change for themselves, the same path will be walked over and over again.

When God took my family from me, that's when I started crying and continued to cry to Him every day. That's how I started believing in Jesus Christ. Sometimes we have to lose everything to find God. Believe me, what God takes away, He will give back twofold or more. All you have to do is be faithful to God. He will bless you in everything.

I have learned to forgive myself and not dwell in the past. I know now that I cannot change what has happened. I can change and continue on the right path for the future, so I can live a much happier life. If I had not forgiven myself, I know I would have fallen back into my old ways.

I cast a spell on my wife a very long time ago. That's one thing that I did not want to let go of because I was scared I would lose my wife. My wife was all I had. I kept praying. After I got saved and confessed all my sins to God, there was one thing that I did not want to let go of and that was the spell on my wife.

Nothing seemed to be working out for me. I started to think that God did not care for me. So, I spoke with my brother Timothy Garcia. He said, "If you want God to work on your life, you have to let go of the spell on your wife, or the Lord will not hear or help you." So, I decided to love God and have faith in Him and let everything go, even my wife and kids. I gave it all to God.

Four days later, I had a dream about killing snakes. I killed three snakes, but I could not kill the big snake, so my wife killed it. Now the Lord is working in me and answering my prayers. Everything seems to be going good. The Lord has given my wife and kids back. My wife started believing in God, and we still have our relationship.

I have not had a mom or dad all my life. Since I have found God, I feel I have a mom and dad because He lives in my heart. He always provides for me even though I do not have any money. He has always given me secondhand blessings. I used to love my wife more than God. Now, God comes first, no matter what. I love God with all my heart. I wish I had met God 29 years ago for I would have been happy all those years like I am now. I want to feel like this for the rest of my life – happy, loved, not worrying, and believing in the true God.

Now things are working for me and my wife because Jesus Christ is in my heart, and He is taking care of my family. All I have to do is be faithful and He will take care of everything for me. God is real. Sometimes He scares me because He can work through people.

Do not be scared to let go of everything for God. Trust God with everything you have and don't worry. Thank you, Jesus, for your love.

13. I CAN CONTINUE TO BE A MESSENGER FOR CHRIST —
Yolanda Martinez

I am here at ACDF on a writ from Arapahoe. I was here in 2006 and got sentenced to community corrections for a burglary charge that I took for someone else. Before I left ACDF, I was a huge warrior for God. I brought a lot of people to Christ. I was released until my sentencing date, but I had to do U.A.'s (urine analysis) and report, kind of like probation.

When I got out, I started staying with my niece. It was the only place I had to go. I knew her mom, but my brother was also staying there, and they were getting high almost every day. It did not bother me too much. I would just walk away. When I went back to court, they sentenced me to 36 months in community corrections. They took me straight to jail from the courtroom. I was devastated because I thought since I was dropping clean UA's for a month, they would be more lenient.

By God's grace, I only waited three days and was sent to the half-way house. I was released to do job search on my birthday, May 1. I was so happy to be back on the streets. I found out I was pregnant with my third child, my second from my current man. My kid's dad had just gotten out of jail. Within three days after getting out, he was already getting high. He would try and get me in trouble because he knew I was in the half-way house. He was very abusive physically, mentally, and emotionally.

I was sent on a furlough from the half-way house and was back at my nieces' home even though I felt it was not a good idea. I had received my first check of $400. My temptation was having money in my pocket. I could have cashed the check and given it directly to the staff. I should have known that the devil had his own plans because I had money. I was starting a new job the next day. My sister-in-law was getting high and I tried to ignore it by going upstairs to sleep. My niece found my sister-in-law's crack pipe and showed me. It was an immediate trigger for me. I had her go buy some dope, then left my niece's house and went on a mission, never to return to the half-way house.

I stayed high for three days. I decided to move out of state with my sister-in-law because she was caring for my other child. I stayed clean for the rest of my pregnancy. My daughter was born December 16, 2006. My kid's dad and my oldest daughter moved out there with me, and we got our life together. He found a really good job, and we had a really nice apartment. We were attending church. My oldest daughter was in high school, although she did not like being in a different state, she still stuck by my side.

We returned to Colorado to visit and started getting high again. After moving back to Colorado, we went downhill fast. I had been on the run for two years and had many encounters with the police, getting away every time. I knew it was my time. I was getting beat up all the time, again. I had a gut feeling I would be arrested soon.

On May 28, 2008, the police showed up at my door. I told my man not to answer the door, but he did anyway. Social Services showed up with the police and said someone had reported drug use. Thank God my children weren't taken away, but they arrested me for escape.

Before I came to Adams County Jail, I was putting off starting a Bible study in Arapahoe County jail. I thought no one would show up, but it turned out excellent. I cannot wait to get back to Arapahoe, so I can continue to be a messenger for Christ.

At ACDF, I was ordered to be held another day so I could go back to court the following morning. I was not very happy because I wanted to get back ASAP. Little did I know that God had a plan. I went to court the following day, then got on a bus with three other ladies. The Holy Spirit spoke to me and told me to ask all the ladies on the bus if they were saved. It felt kind of weird, because I did not know any of them. I'm learning to listen to the Holy Spirit. I knew it was not my voice. I felt my heart fill with joy when the Holy Spirit spoke to me. So, I just blurted it out, "Are you all saved?" Two answered, "Yes" and one answered, "No." I left it at that. I did not say anymore. When it was time to go to court, the woman who answered "No," was in the same courtroom as me. We were locked in a cell by ourselves. She started crying, and again the Holy Spirit spoke to me and said, "This is your chance!" I prayed with her and immediately she stopped crying. Thank you Holy Spirit! Amen!

I received two years at DOC for my sentence in the half-way house and one year for escape. I need to learn to listen to the Holy Spirit more. I felt in my heart that I should never have furloughed to my niece's. I was so anxious about leaving the half-way house for the weekend, that I thought I could handle anything. Now, I'm back doing time. I do not mind because I know I'm forgiven. I am on track, following and getting to know my Lord once again.

My children and I are safe and healthy, and I know I'm not causing my Lord grief! I am currently fighting for custody of my three children. Social Services spoke with someone and knew of the domestic violence that had occurred two days prior to my arrest. My children were devastated, and they were on my mind constantly.

I had a dream and saw my Mom (who has been deceased for ten years) in this really beautiful church. I saw one of my kids on her lap and the other one sitting next to her. It was like an out-of-body experience. I could see them, but they could not see me, and I was unable to say anything. It was God's way of letting me know my kids were okay. But see, the devil comes to steal, kill, and destroy. The next night I had a dream that only one of my kids was with my Mom, and I could not find my youngest one. I woke up in a bad sweat. I believe the devil was trying to steal my happiness! He was lying to me to make me believe my children weren't okay.

I recently went to court and my oldest child was placed with her step-mom and the other two were placed with my husband's sister. I thank you dear God for watching over my kids. Now the Holy Spirit is telling me to stop focusing on them and start focusing on God. Without Him, I wouldn't have my kids! And without Him, I can never be the mother to my children that they deserve. This is a big eye opener for me because I know that without God, I will end up lost and without my children in my life. I will end up in emotional hell! Please pray for me, as I will for all who read my story.

14. A FRIEND'S APOLOGY — Randy Palmer

I met C in my pod, and even though he was with us only a short period of time, I got to hear a lot about his family, kids and his struggles. This man had a smile on his face, a grin from ear to ear. He was always a very giving man.

One day he only had one Ramen noodle left for the week, and someone had asked him if he had any. Instead of being like most people, selfish or saying "No, this is my last one, I cannot do anything for you," C just gave it to the man for nothing in return. One day, he even shared his last oatmeal cream pie while talking about his family. He was always giving and never expecting anything in return. You do not meet many people like that, and when you do, it's a blessing from God.

C seemed to have lots of struggles, and one night another brother and I thought C was trying to take his life. When we asked him, he replied, "I promise I won't do it. I'll talk to you about it in the morning." So, we told him, "Okay, we'll trust you but first let's pray." We prayed for him.

The next morning, I found out that C had taken his life. It tore me apart inside. For days and days I cried, and for the longest time I really could not sleep well. I thought his death was in a way my fault. Even though C had given me his word that he was not going to do it, I could not stop him.

Then two or three nights after C passed away, I had a dream about him. C told me that he was sorry for taking his life. To me that dream was very meaningful because he was a very good friend. The Lord gave me that dream as a chance for C to say he was sorry for lying to me and taking his life. "Thank you, Lord, for that dream! Thank you for helping me see C in spirit and for giving me peace."

I can truly say that God has sent me to this jail for a reason. I also believe that I have been blessed to be placed in B Module. I am growing stronger in my faith. God gave me a few people to be in my life so I can grow stronger in my faith. Jesus has done this for me.

I have been self-conscious about being put up on stage, or speaking on anything. I've always been the one to sit quietly, in the back, watch what was going on, and listen to what others said. I never say a word. I would always wonder what other people would say, think, or do to me for what I would say. I especially wondered about the people I knew. What would they do if I were to give them the Jesus talk? I was scared of what they would do to me.

Since I have been here, my brothers in faith have gotten me to admit this to them; well, Jesus has. Slowly and steadily for the last 45 days, I have asked God to help me. I prayed to the Lord, "Jesus, help me. Help me to get over my stage fright. Help me to speak up." Jesus heard my prayer, and He answered it.

So far, I have led our prayer group for Bible study once. I have prayed one-on-one with my brothers before they went to court. I've led prayers on many occasions. Then on May 2, 2008, I asked God to help me lead a prayer in the holding tank for people I do not know. I was taking a bigger step in faith. On that occasion I did not lead a prayer for everyone. Jesus pointed me to a special soul in need. This man had about eight felonies and was looking at 16–48 years in prison.

The Holy Spirit picked me up, told me to walk over, and try to calm and ease his spirit. I asked him if he believed in our Lord Jesus Christ. He said, "Yeah, kinda. Why?" I asked him to share the salvation prayer with me. He did, and asked me, "How can I have faith, looking at so much time?" I told him, "Let's pray on it." Right then, the deputy came in and called him out to see the judge. I told him to hold onto his faith and to trust in God and leave it in His hands. He left the holding cell with tears in his eyes, saying, "I will, I will." The man came back with a smile on his face; the Lord had worked His grace. Our Lord put it on the D.A.'s and judge's hearts to drop all eight felonies and give him a "misdemeanor one or two." This man is free today. Praise the Lord!

To me, that was the first small big step He gave me in getting over my stage fright and problem with speaking up. Then the Lord gave me one of the biggest steps I have ever taken. Early morning, May 7, I was going to court for sentencing. I was not too worried about what was going to happen to me, I had put it in God's hands. What I did was pray to our Lord Jesus Christ to help me speak up in the holding cell, so that I might win over as many souls for Him as I could.

I'm pleased to share with you, there were lots of people in the holding cell. First, I was hesitant to speak up. However, I thought, "No, I gotta speak up." The Holy Spirit gave me strength to speak. I started when there was a silent moment. I said, "Is anyone going for sentencing today? No, scratch that. Who would like to say a prayer with me?" Everyone said, "Yeah," and bowed their heads and let me pray for them.

God is good. He has answered my prayers. I'm over my stage

fright. I'm finally able to speak up and out. Praise the Lord! As you can see, God has now gotten me up on stage, speaking out to you, writing a testimony and sharing it with you. God is good and God is great. I have now learned to thank Him for all things and everyone in my life. I thank the Lord for my older brother Lonnie and my other brothers. Thank you, Lord Jesus our Savior, from your servant, Randy Palmer. I love you.

15. I AM NO LONGER LOST — Gino Hinojosa

Looking back on my life of gangs, drugs, and crime, I remember that even from a very young age, Jesus was calling me. All of my life, whether I was in jail or out in the world, strangers would come up to me out of nowhere, tell me how Jesus loves me and how He can save me. I just was not ready. I thought I was in control of my life. Boy, was I wrong. I had no control. I was a slave to sin!

At age seven, I took my first hit of grass. At age nine, I tasted my first drink of alcohol and received my first tattoo. At age 12, after being caught driving my motorcycle on the streets of Denver late one night, I was brought home by the police officer who stopped me. After searching me, he found a straight razor, one ounce of grass and an empty coke seal. He told my mom everything that he had found and that I was headed for big trouble. Then, he put me in the back of the car. I thought I was going to jail, but instead he started telling me about Jesus and how He loved me. Of course I listened – anything to avoid jail.

At the age of 16, while most kids were learning how to play football, I had a needle in my arm and had experienced juvenile hall. I was in lockup without a clue where my life was headed. Coming from a poor, dysfunctional, broken home of five, in a rough east Denver neighborhood, I took to the streets, gangs, and drugs to escape the reality of being abused. I totally lost contact with who I was or why I was in this world. Little did I know I would spend the next twenty years battling the demons of addiction. It left me spending all of my 20's and 30's in and out of prison; 15 of those years were on the inside.

When all is said and done, I've always been tough. Something I learned at a young age on the streets and in juvenile hall. Going to church and talking about God was always a sign of weakness in my eyes. I sure did not need God. I was tough with over 200 pounds of attitude and the capability for extreme violence. I knew it all and had seen it all; guns and shootouts, knives and stabbings, needles and overdoses, smiles and tears.

I have lost so much over the years; wives, children, and all the material things this world has to offer. I had given up on ever being a normal, caring, and loving man. I figured I would end up dead or in prison for the rest of my life. I was hopeless and did not even know it. I knew I was lost; I did not know how to get back to normal.

On April 27, 2005, I had been given parole and another chance. I met the most beautiful woman and fell in love. My children and family were in my life with their love and full support. I started subcontracting electrical jobs. But, I was doing it Gino's way. I had forgotten that my way was always the wrong way! I thought all I had was not enough. I wanted more women, more money, and more of this big pie that I felt was owed to me. Once again, I started using drugs and losing myself. When I looked up, everything I had gained was lost.

On November 5, 2005, I was charged with attempted murder and sent to jail. I was kicking drugs. I lost my girl, my children, my life, my home, my business and my car. I was in a cell, knowing I would never get out of prison, but if I did I would be too old to care. My life had just ended. I had hit rock bottom so many times before. I knew what it felt like. I even had a system for dealing with it. This time it would be different and more intense than I ever could imagine.

I broke down once again, and there was no coming out of this one! I found myself unable to stop crying. The pain of what was going on was a hundred times worse than I remembered. I was in total despair: hopeless, lost, in such pain. All I could do was cry myself to sleep. I would eat, go back to my cell, crawl under the desk or bed, and wail at the top of my lungs, pleading with God, "GOD, PLEASE HELP ME! O GOD, PLEASE HELP ME!" The guards and my cellie thought I was dying. I thought I was already dead.

Then I fell into a deep sleep, and God came to me. In my dream, I was on my knees in some dirt in a place I had never been before. I was crying, and I felt what I thought was rain on my head. I looked up and right in front of me was Jesus on the cross. He was crying and the blood from His hand was dripping on my head. He looked down at me with tears in His eyes. He told me my life was wrong in God's eyes and that I should repent and change my ways. He said He loved me. He asked me to take His hand and follow Him. If not, He would come when I least expected it, and I would not be ready. He told me to choose. I chalked all this up to hallucinations from kicking drugs. I had this dream every time I went to sleep for the next three days.

On the third day, in a cold cell, I surrendered my life to Jesus. I have not been the same since. I have been delivered from being a slave to Satan. The last offer from the district attorney was 20 to 32 years if I would plead out to first degree assault with a deadly weapon while on parole. I went to trial. I was found guilty of second degree assault in a crime of passion which carries one to three years. Jesus has truly saved me! I was not supposed to walk out of here this time. Now I am saved. Jesus has been there all along for me! All I had to do was turn to Him, lean on Him, trust in Him, and believe in Him.

I look back on all the times strangers and people would tell me about Jesus and God. One time in 1992, I was working for MCI calling people from state to state to ask whether they would like to change to MCI from AT&T. I was hooked on coke and heroin. I called a family in California and the guy at the other end told me how he only allowed one phone in his home because he was a Christian and one was all he needed. He told me how he had been hooked on heroin, spent 10 years in prison and gave his life to Jesus. He had been clean for 10 years and now has a great life. This guy did not know me, and yet he told me that he knew that I had called him for a reason. He asked if we could pray over the phone. I did not want to disrespect him, so I agreed. He prayed that Jesus would come to me and open my eyes. He knew something was wrong. He asked me what was going on. I told him that I could not say, and he told me the only way out was Jesus.

Fifteen years later, I look back and see how right he was. How lost I was. How Jesus has saved me from death so many times. I'm so thankful to be alive and healthy. My number one priority in life is to find out what God's will is for me. I cannot be free, I cannot be a father, I cannot be a husband, and I cannot be a member of society without God. I am a nobody who wants to tell everybody about somebody who can save anybody! I should have listened long before, but I was too hard-headed and my heart was hardened. God Himself had to come to me so I would surrender to His plan for my life. He has saved me, cleansed me, and now I am a new man in Christ!

It's really something to see the absolute joy on the faces of people who knew me before. They see what God has done to me. They do not even recognize me. The pain, shame, guilt, hatred, and anger are gone. I've been delivered from drug addiction, alcoholism, and sin. We all still struggle with sin, but being saved gives us the strength through Jesus to overcome sin. We are victorious in Jesus and His blood on the cross at Calvary.

I've been freed after 30 years of being a slave to sin. Now, I'm a bond servant to Jesus Christ. Now I am free! I've totally surrendered my life to the will of God. I witness to everyone who will listen. I love to serve God. I keep it real. I'm a Christian in the pod, in the yard, in my cell, and in the shower! I stay in the Word of God and pray diligently. I have fallen in love with Jesus because He came to me, saving me, loving me, and caring for me when I did not even love myself. It's tough sometimes. It's not easy picking up my cross daily and following Jesus. It's an on-going process, not an event! I know I can trust in God's love and plan for me. I'm no longer lost! Praise God! (This story was first printed in the book, *Maximum Saints Make No Little Plans.)*

16. GOD MADE ME A MINISTER — Dennis Gibbons

My father was a minister and my mother was a missionary. They came from Ohio. My parents made me go to church at least four days a week, and in the summertime, I had to attend Bible school all summer.

When I was young, I used to play preach to mock the preachers. When I turned 18, I went to a revival meeting and gave my life to the Lord. That day, the Lord spoke to me and said, "This day is for you to be saved." Later that day I went to a friend's house and prayed to receive the Holy Spirit. Then I was filled with the Holy Spirit and started speaking in tongues.

Soon after that I had a dream. I was preaching in a big church for the Lord and not mocking God. I did not read the Bible in those days, though I had faith in God. I backslid and turned to living in the world, like I'd never known the Lord. I started selling drugs and running from the Lord, doing things not of God, moving from place to place and city to city.

Once, I ended up in prison and hit rock bottom. I called on Jesus and rededicated my life to Him. I started reading the Bible and understanding came to me immediately. I started encouraging other people to read the Word of God. So many years later, I am totally sold out to the Lord, preaching and teaching His word daily. Also, the Lord has blessed ACDF with a strong prayer minister who is powerful in changing many people's lives.

During my time here at ACDF, the Lord has allowed me to train in ministry. I have been able to help many other people and lead them to the Lord. Lately, I had another dream about preaching. It's been 25 years since I had my last preaching dream. This time, the Lord showed a few faces that I will never forget. He allowed me to pray over these people. In the dream, the place was so big, I was in awe!! There were rivers of people in front of me. This was a vision within my dream. I asked, "Why Lord? Why did you choose me?" I did not feel worthy. The Lord said to me, "I made you a minister." I replied, "Yes, Lord, yes, Lord." Now I preach in the chaplain's worship services, and that's God's grace. I would not change this for anything in the world.

My advice to whoever reads this testimony is that you just need to trust in the Lord with all your heart, mind, soul, and strength. You will never be wrong for making this decision. Paul wrote, *"Now to Him who is able to do immeasurably more than all we ask or imagine, according to his power that is at work within us, to him be glory in the church and in Christ Jesus throughout all generations, forever and ever! Amen."* (Ephesians 3:20-21)

17. ALL THINGS WORK TOGETHER FOR GOOD EVEN CANCER — Vickie Montoya

I was 28 years old and had just finished doing a year sentence at Jeffco. The month before my release, though, I started bleeding very badly, clumps of blood, and I waited until my release to see the doctor. Bad move! By the time I had seen the nurse I was bleeding so badly they could not do a pap smear. She sent me immediately to St. Joseph Hospital. I was diagnosed with stage B cervical cancer. I started radiation and chemotherapy immediately. It was too late to do a hysterectomy because the tumor had already spread to my lymph nodes.

I had to give up my job and move back home with my grandparents. My grandpa drove me to the hospital every day to get radiation treatments, and three times a week for chemotherapy. I had to do this for six weeks. After all this treatment I had to do one final procedure. It was a "live or die" radiation treatment. It was very experimental, but if I survived I would be cancer free. For 72 hours – three days – I could have no visits. The radiation was so much that not even the nurses could come in to give me medicine. That is why they had me on a morphine button.

I fell asleep and I believe I died for a short time. All I do know for sure is I went down this tunnel of memories. All the events in my life were before me like a movie. I was not just observing it, I was feeling all the pain, joy, envy, love as well as all the emotions I brought on others. I felt what they had felt. I had to feel the pain my grandma felt when I ran away from home at 12 years old. I had to feel the pain of my kids when they could not come home with me at the visits – all of it.

At the end of this tunnel was a bright light. When I reached it I felt this overwhelming feeling that all was how it was supposed to be and that everything was going to be okay. God forgave me and gave me a choice – to stay or to come back. I came back a totally different person. I learned the biggest lesson of my life: 1) Love God more than anything; 2) Treat people the way you want to be treated, no matter how they treat you.

God loves us so much I cannot explain it. It's something you have to feel and I believe someday we all will completely understand His love and His plan. Until then, we just need to try to be good and always love God. This is my favorite testimony. Of course, none of us are capable of following the rules above without the power of the Lord in our lives. When Jesus saves us, he changes us from being self -centered to God/others-centered people! Paul wrote, *"Therefore, if anyone is in Christ, he is a new creation; the old has gone, the new has come!" (2 Corinthians 5:17)*

18. DO NOT TURN YOUR BACK ON HIM — Jose Garcia

One Sunday, I told the chaplain I was going to give my testimony at chaplain's worship in two weeks. But in those two weeks I lost my wife to the world of her deception and cheating with another man. Coming here to worship, I was grieving for the loss of someone who was very dear to me. I was having second thoughts about giving my testimony. I searched within myself, and I asked my God to give me the strength to go up there and tell my story.

I've been coming in and out of jail, procrastinating in giving my life to my Lord Jesus Christ. Whenever I was released, I would go back to the devil's work. My drug, rock cocaine, was destroying my life. I was dragging my wife down with me as I manipulated her to get more drugs.

The last time I was incarcerated for domestic violence in the beginning of November 2001, again I surrendered my life to my God: receiving the Holy Spirit and also receiving the gift of healing with prayer. My brother had been diagnosed with colon cancer, and I prayed for him to be healed. The next day he was in remission. Thanks be to God!

But I did not really understand about the Holy Spirit. I was arrested again on the charge of domestic violence, let out on bail, and still chose to get lost in the world of destruction. I was still smoking rock cocaine, not knowing when to quit. I was causing arguments with my wife about money problems, but I was not motivated to work it out. I did not listen to my wife when she was crying out to me to stop what I was doing. I landed in jail again, picked up by undercover cops for failure to appear. Coming to jail, in F1100, I saw my brother-in-law. I knew him out in the free world. I saw him so differently this time, as though there was a bright light over him. Then he told me, "I was waiting for you." I asked, "How did you know I was coming?" He said, "The Lord told me!" He had given his life to God.

The next morning I was looking for him, and he was going to different cubicles, getting different Scriptures from different people. I sat down to listen, still thinking of getting out and doing my drug.

Then he asked me, "Do you want a Bible? I have an extra." I replied, "No, I am getting out in two or three months." Then he said, "Do not put off until tomorrow what you could do today!" So then I took the Bible and got back into the Word. I was anxious to get where I had been the last time.

I had given my life to the Lord and had been going to church every Saturday. I was learning about Pentecost, the Holy Spirit, and my spiritual condition. By choosing to meditate on Scriptures, applying them to our lives and following God's standard for our thinking, we will live in a way that pleases the Father. We will become the people He planned for us to be and accomplish His purposes for us.

My communication with my God grew stronger. In the Bible it says to be honest and truthful with yourself and others. *"Then you will know the truth, and the truth will set you free." (John 8:32)* I was in denial about my drug habit. But when I read that verse, I started to open up about my drug problem and work on it. I started to go to classes like Drug Ed., N.A., and so forth. God knows everything and sees everything. I was hiding my addiction from the courts, but not any more. I want to be set free not only from jail, but also from my own destruction.

I started to work on my character. One area I knew I had to work on was my impatience. I needed to be healed of an old wound received from a past relationship. I was using the drugs to numb my pain caused by my wife in the past. This got me even closer to my God. I gave Him all my pain, worries, stress – my everything. Turning it all over to God, I gave Him my whole life.

Then one night in a vision, I saw a demon in one of my peers, and the devil was telling me, "I want you. You are mine." I was scared and I rebuke the devil in the name of Jesus. He is not wanted here. Covering my head with my blanket in fear, I felt tears coming down my face. My God called on me, and He said, "Do not fear, I am here, my son." I had already received the Holy Spirit, but I did not understand it. In that moment I did. I felt such peace, joy, contentment, and was very happy. I asked my God to forgive me for all my sins and to cleanse me. He then told me that I had the gift of healing with prayer. The Holy Spirit would teach me how to use the gift in the right way since I have immense compassion for others.

When I came to jail this time, I was changing my life so my wife wouldn't leave me, but now I am changing for me. I was beating myself down before. I thought it was all my fault, but now I see things more clearly. Yes, I have some faults, but I have to learn from my mistakes and own them, so I won't stumble over the same faults again. I give thanks to my God for staying by me all the way. God is always there if you call on him. He never deserts you. He loves you. Do not turn your back on Him. When I get released and walk out of this place, I am going to walk out with my head up and with my Lord Jesus Christ right next to me. (This story was first published in the book, *Maximum Saints Make No Little Plans*.)

19. THE OFFER — Elizabeth Davalos

It was late at night and I was thinking to myself and said, "I would give anything just to get my freedom back." I had been in prison for three years already. I was still getting high on pills. I had just gotten out of the hole for overdosing on pills. Well, when I got out, I was thinking about how to get my next high. I fell asleep and Satan came to me in my dreams. He showed me all kinds of things that I wanted: money, drugs, alcohol, cars and everything you could possibly think. He said, "You could have all these and your freedom if you come with me." He also showed me my family, my parents, brothers, sisters and my children. They were crying.

He said, "The only thing you can never have or see is your family." I felt this big loss in my heart but then I kept hearing my sister-in-law, Rosario, who passed away. I kept hearing her say to me, "Snap out of it. Snap out of it, Lisa." My family calls me Lisa. So I told Satan, "No I won't go with you. I want my family." Then I woke up from my dream. It had been so real. I believe in reality what Satan was asking me was real.

I put my Bible under my head in my pillow because every time I would try to go to sleep, I could feel Satan wanting to get me. He wouldn't give up. I stood firm and prayed while he tried to confuse me because for a minute, I could not remember how to pray. Then I rebuked him in the name of Lord Jesus Christ and Satan left.

I think if I would have left with Satan, I would be dead or doing really bad things. I am happy to know that Jesus loves me and that He set me free.

20. A MESSAGE FROM GOD — Anita Lopez

I came to ACDF on May 2, 2008, for violation of probation. Although I considered myself to be a good mother, in reality I was not. I've been a drug user for about ten years. I started using crack cocaine when I was about 16 years old. I had my two younger children well after I had my daughter who is now 13 years old. My daughter did not like the fact that I used drugs. I was aware of that, but I continued using.

My daughter first ran away when she was 11 years old. It was the worst feeling I have ever felt when she came home. I screamed at her and called her just about every name in the book. I only did what I've been taught by my mother. She was never able to show love physically or mentally. I can remember that much.

On July 4, I called my mother. She was caring for my three children at the time. She told me that my daughter had run away again and it had already been a week. I was serving a six-month sentence. I was devastated. One month went by, and still my daughter was not home. Two months went by, and by that time, I was losing my mind knowing there was nothing I could do to help find her. I could only pray. One night I went to church and gave myself to the Lord. I was born again and I cried so much I felt like a two-year-old child.

I asked my Father God, "Please take care of my daughter. Please let her be safe. Let no harm come to her." That night I had a dream. I was walking down a street knocking on all the doors asking them for my daughter. I got to the corner house and a woman answered. I asked, "Is my daughter here?" She replied, "Come in." So I went in and sat down. She was talking to a man while I waited. She turned to me and said, "No, I have not seen her." Then someone knocked on the door. When the woman opened it, my daughter was standing there. My daughter said, "Mom, grandma told me to come and tell you that I'm home now." My daughter was beautiful. I saw beautiful light that shown about her and it made me feel at ease. I started screaming at her calling her names and then suddenly she disappeared. I believe God spoke to me through my dream that my daughter is okay and is at home. Also, God was telling me to stop speaking to her that way. God knew I needed to break the chain of sinful behaviors which were passed through generations.

I called my Mom the following day and my daughter answered the phone. I was so happy. I did not scream or curse at her. I just cried. I told her I was glad she was home and wished I could be there to give her a big hug and kiss. So you see, God does speak to us through our dreams. God bless you all.

21. REFLECTIONS ON A PRAYER PROJECT — Demond High

The Prayer Project on "How to Listen to God's Voice" has been a great inspiration to my whole life and relationship with God. Before I got started, my prayer life was good, but I knew that there was something missing. I had a lot of questions like: Does God really hear my prayers? Does God truly forgive me? How do I know God's will or when God is speaking to me? Well, I found out the reason I had so many questions is because I was doing all the talking.

I would constantly pray day after day asking God a lot of things but never giving Him a chance to respond. I addressed this issue with Chaplain McDonald, and she suggested that I should try a prayer project, "How to Listen to God's Voice." I decided to give it a try! My assignment was to spend one hour with the Lord every day, 30 minutes in His word, 15 minutes in prayer talking to God and 15 minutes in listening.

Through doing this, I have experienced a miracle. I would pray for 15 minutes and then listen. God began to speak to my heart and mind. I know that it was God because it was not things that I usually told myself. It was all positive things that could change my life. God says in His word that His sheep hear His voice and a stranger's voice we will not follow. *"When he has brought out all his own, he goes on ahead of them, and his sheep follow him because they know his voice. But they will never follow a stranger; in fact, they will run away from him because they do not recognize a stranger's voice." (John 10:4-5)*

I continued to pray each day. My prayer life and relationship with God has been greatly enriched. I love God, speaking to Him and Him speaking to me. There is nothing more important than getting closer to our Creator, Savior, and Lord. I trust in the promises of His Word, which is also His voice. All of my prayers have been answered! I have prayed for God's blessings in my life, for my family, friends, and enemies.

Prior to this prayer project, I also participated on another prayer project called, From "The Flood of Incarceration" to "The Flood of Revival" My prayer for revival of the incarcerated was answered. The pod I am in was very loud. Nobody was attending church or praying, plus there was a lot of negativity. Praise God! All that has changed, now more people are going to church, less negativity, not as loud, and, to top it off, we have a continuously growing prayer circle every night.

God is good, isn't He! Also, a lot of Bible study is going on. Some who did not believe are beginning to respond to the powerful life-changing message in His Word. Hallelujah! I started another Prayer Project called "Healing from Nightmares." I am already experiencing victory! I know now more than ever that prayer works. Enjoying God's presence has become a daily desire for me. Prayer for me is no longer only a project, but a very enjoyable, fulfilling lifestyle, and I continue to pray in Jesus' name. Amen.

22. DISCOVERY OF MAXIMUM SAINTS — Chaplain McDonald

I have encountered many powerful spiritual leaders at ACDF. I call these treasured saints, "Maximum Saints." Maximum Saints are not necessarily classified as maximum security inmates, rather, classified by using their gifts to the maximum to help others.

Many Maximum Saints have made a great positive impact in our facility. These saints create peace, hope, and healing through the message of Christ in the midst of pain, suffering, and turmoil. Also, they are making a difference by sharing their stories of transformation through Maximum Saints books and DVDs which are distributed in jails, prisons, and homeless shelters nationwide, free of charge when chaplains or volunteers request them.

The outside world does not even realize that these incarcerated saints exist. I feel privileged to meet these saints, and I want the outside people to know how they are making a difference. In each Maximum Saints book, I mentioned some extraordinary saints. I have met many Maximum Saints, but I would like to mention Jonathan Willis, 25 years old. I thanked God for Jonathan many times. It was a privilege and honor to meet him even though his time here at ACDF was brief.

When I first met Jonathan, he was in a maximum security

pod in A Module. I asked for someone to lead the song in one of the chaplain's worship services. Everyone pointed at Jonathan. Jonathan, a song writer and singer, shared his testimony and sermons in chaplain's worship services. His story was published in the second ACDF incarcerated saints' book, *Maximum Saints Make No Little Plans*, and titled, "Fear Within Us."

One day, Jonathan wanted to speak with a chaplain because he was concerned about his case. He had a difficult time focusing on serving the Lord at the time. This has changed since he moved to B Module. I saw the transformation in him. He looked happier after he started leading the Bible study and the prayer circle in his pod. He was very effective and his influence was powerful.

When the Transformation Project Prison Ministry (TPPM) was ready to make the second Maximum Saints DVD, I asked Jonathan to be a part of this project with his song and testimony. I was amazed by his enthusiasm and his talents, and I felt blessed by his contribution. He said he kept writing songs without knowing how God could be able to help him use them.

Then one day Jonathan wanted to see me. I knew his trial was coming up. Before he shared his struggles, I told him he did not have to tell me anything, but that he should obey what God was telling him to do to find peace. He agreed. He knew what God wanted him to do was tell the truth. He knew telling the truth would be costly and he may not ever be freed, but he followed what God told him to do. He pled guilty and was sentenced to life without parole.

After his sentencing, I went to visit him. I expected that he would come out with a stressed, gloomy, sad, and depressed look on his face. I was wrong. Jonathan had a big smile and shared how he felt good about telling the truth, because that's what God wanted him to do. He shared that he was ready to serve the Lord for the rest of his life in prison. He also said, "Chaplain, I received a letter from Adam's mom, and it encouraged me so much. All I am going through is worth it when I think about the letter. I will do anything to receive letters like that." Adam was an inmate in Jonathan's pod.

The next time I visited, Jonathan sang a song for me and my assistant. It almost made me cry. I was so touched. We went there to comfort and encourage Jonathan. Instead, he was ministering to us. I knew there was hope. He knows how to turn misery into joy by finding purpose in life. He found joy in an impossible situation by making a commitment to serve the Lord for the rest of his life.

As we were talking, Jonathan said somehow he remembered what he used to pray. His prayer was to be a missionary, and he said he will be a missionary for the Lord in prison. A couple of days later, I remembered Jonathan's comment about Adam's mom's letter. I asked if he could share it with me. He told me he had already mailed the letter to his Mom the night before. While I was talking with him, a mail lady was picking up the mail. Jonathan ran to her and got the letter and shared it with me.

Here is part of the letter from Adam's mom. She gave TPPM permission to add her letter here.

Dear Jonathan,

Hi, I am Adam's mom. I wanted to write to you to tell you, "Thank you so much for being the messenger I prayed for." I had asked our Heavenly Father to send Adam a messenger in jail to speak His word to him, and in my heart I believe you are that messenger.

I have never heard my son so humble, and speaking of our Lord so gracefully. You have been a blessing to him. He tells me how much he sees the Holy Spirit within you. Please continue to use what our Heavenly Father has given you, which is a soft spirit to preach His word to the lost.

Jesus is coming for His church very, very soon. You remind me of Paul in the Bible. He wrote most of the New Testament. Be strong and listen to His voice, for you are on the path to win souls for the kingdom, and your rewards will be great in heaven. I'm praying for you.

I would like to continue to write to you and send some sermons your way from our pastor. Please write back and give me your address to where they are sending you. Be strong and know that there are brothers and sisters in Christ praying with and for you. God bless you. Adam's mom

I reread the letter in tears and thanked God for Jonathan. Before Jonathan left our facility, he shared with me that in prison there is a job program in which he could make some money. When he does that, he would send the money to support the TPPM. This touched me deeply because he is the one who needs it more, but he was thinking about others.

Though Jonathan has left ACDF, his legacy lives on. One day I was leading worship in A Module, and I asked inmates to share their stories of transformation and what the turning points were for them. One inmate shared how he met Jonathan Willis in B Module. He mentioned how Jonathan, who had received a life sentence, was calm, peaceful, and witnessed to others. This encouraged him. He shared that he accepted Christ and decided to change his gang life because of him. This man also added that he was baptized by me one day in B Module because Jonathan had shared Christ with him. Then I remembered the day when Jonathan was sitting next to this man, telling me how this man accepted the Lord and wanted to be baptized. Before Jonathan left, he gave him a study Bible that he had received from his mother. This man opened the Bible showing where Jonathan's name was.

One day I got a phone call from a reporter at the Denver Post newspaper who wanted to know more about the TPPM. He explained that he was writing an article about jail conversion and how real it is. I told him it is real. Many incarcerated people are hurting but God is blessing many people who are open to Him. He asked me what makes me believe that Christianity has the answer to transformation. I told him that Christian belief offers a spiritual map, good morals, direction like loving God, loving others, and has the path to transformation through Jesus Christ. I have seen many transformed lives through Christianity that I have not seen through any other religion. The reporter told me he was interviewing people by visiting different facilities and ministry settings. The reporter came to our facility and interviewed some inmates and also went to interview Jonathan who already moved to another facility. God reminded me that He is honored when people share their stories of transformation in Christ. *"They overcame him by the blood of the Lamb and by the word of their testimony; they did not love their lives so much as to shrink from death." (Rev 12:11)*

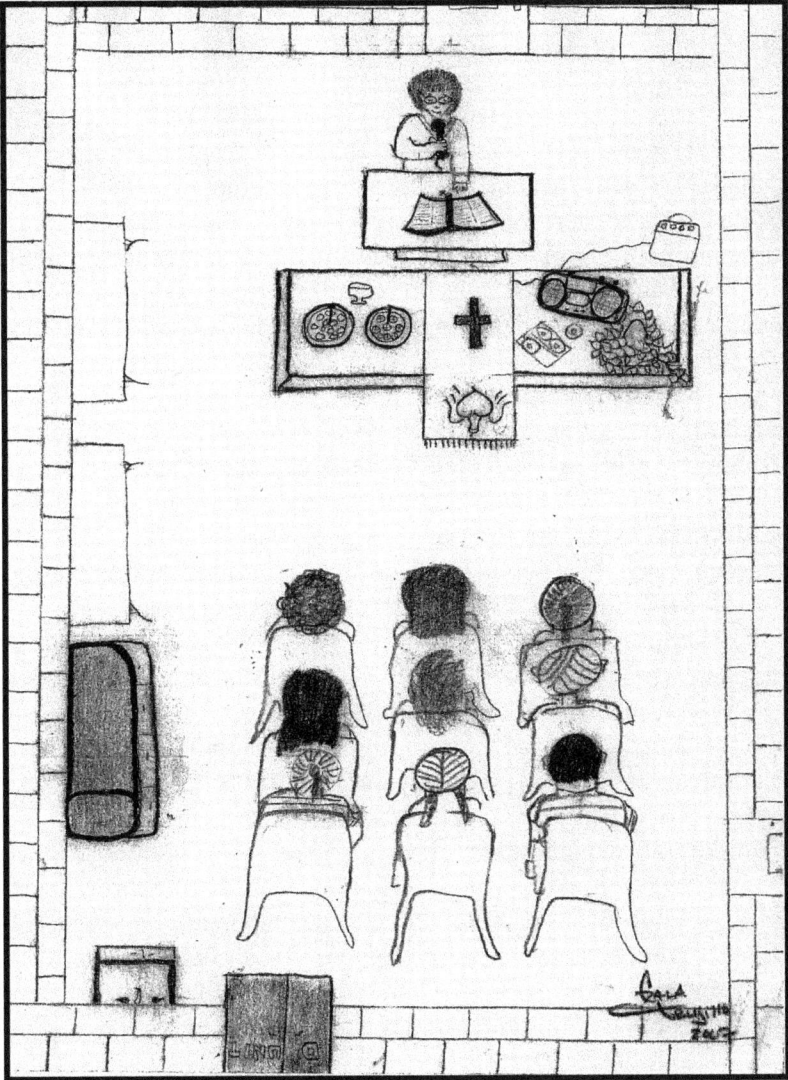

"Chaplain's Worship Service" by an ACDF inmate

Part Two:
Questions Concerning Dreams

by Chaplain McDonald
Edited by Michael Goins

People are often confused or puzzled by their dreams because they make no sense or are frightening. I encourage everyone who reads this book to start journaling their dreams and to ask God for an interpretation of them to remove confusion and misunderstanding about the meaning. It will help broaden your understanding and help you understand how God uses dreams to communicate with us.

God can and does speak to us through our dreams. He can and will help us interpret our dreams if only we ask, wait, and patiently listen. Not all dreams come from God, some come from the devil. Some dreams are affected by what you are exposed to, movies you watch, habits you have, medication you take or trauma you have gone through. What we dream may also be related to stress. Each dream can teach you about your spiritual condition and it can help you understand how to rely on God to find peace in your heart.

The practice of listening to God's voice will help you distinguish whether a dream is from God or from others. Dreams are simply one avenue that God uses to speak to us. The more you learn to quiet your mind and ask God to give you wisdom, knowledge, and revelation to understand your dreams, the more you will learn to recognize His voice.

For those who suffer from nightmares, I encourage you to follow a 30-Day Prayer Project, "Healing from Nightmares," which is in Part Four of this book, until you find peace, strength, and confidence in your heart or are no longer afraid to go to sleep. If you still suffer from nightmares when you finish the 30-Day Prayer Project, start over again until you are healed from them.

The following are some frequently asked questions from ACDF inmates concerning dreams. My answers come from my own understanding of the Scripture concerning dreams, as well as reflections on my own dreams.

1. <u>Why do we dream?</u> — I believe God created sleep for us to rest, and also for us to dream. We may not always remember what we dream, and there are times that we may not dream at all. The Bible talks about dreams as one of the ways God communicates with us. Daniel, Jacob, Mary, Joseph, and many others had dreams, and they understood their meanings. In the books of Joel and Acts, the Scriptures tell us that one of the signs of the outpouring of the Holy Spirit is dreaming. *(Acts 2:17-18)* According to this Scripture, a dream is a gift, which means not everyone receives it.

2. <u>Why do we dream the same dream again and again?</u> — A recurring dream may imply that there's a message we have not figured out yet. In these: (1) God may be trying to tell us something, and we need to clear our mind and listen to God to understand it; (2) we may need to take care of something in our life, and God may be trying to point it out to us; or, (3) you may have been traumatized by an event in your life, and you need healing. Reflect and see if there is any unfinished business in your life. If God is asking you to take care of something, obey Him by letting it go, forgiving or reconciling if you can. Each of us has a mental "filing cabinet" containing many different files. Sometimes they overflow or become disorganized. Ask the Holy Spirit which part you need to take care of and then obey Him. For those who have Post Traumatic Stress Disorder (PTSD), pray to God to heal your memories so you can release them.

3. <u>Why do my dreams feel so real?</u> — Our hearts (emotions) and minds (intellect) are engaged in our dreams; therefore dreams can seem real at times and at other times they do not. If there is a specific reason why your dreams seem so real, God will know why – ask Him!

4. <u>I dream that my boyfriend is hanging out with other women or people that he knows I do not like. What does that mean?</u> — You need to ask God for understanding and ask Him for peace of mind. You cannot control other people, but with God's help you can control your mind. Perhaps God is telling you about what is happening now or may happen in the future, or perhaps the dream could actually be revealing your own insecurity in your

relationship. Ask Him to give you wisdom to handle whatever comes your way, including your relationships.

5. <u>Is it okay to interpret our own dreams</u>? — I encourage everyone to learn how to interpret dreams. Ask God for interpretations and you will be amazed when you finally learn to recognize His voice. When we try to interpret our own dreams we might be confused, but when God speaks to us everything becomes clear. The Holy Spirit will confirm what you have learned from your dream, but it takes time to quiet your mind and listen.

6. <u>Why do we have bad dreams or nightmares</u>? — There are many reasons why we have nightmares, but we can overcome them with God's help. I can think of nine reasons or circumstances for nightmares:

(1) When we are physically, mentally, emotionally and/or spiritually weak and stressed, the devil can take advantage of those moments with nightmares, especially if you are gifted with spiritual discernment. People who have that gift can feel, see, or hear the spiritual world. Sometimes they can feel the devil's attack in dreams as well as when they are awake.

(2) If we are under a lot of stress, suffering or in pain, we might experience bad dreams. Traumatized people are more vulnerable. The devil takes advantage of the situation when we are hurting.

(3) When we cannot control our minds and our hearts we are also vulnerable. The devil tries to control our minds when we are under the influence of alcohol, drugs, and even prescription drugs, not only when we are awake, but also while we are asleep. When the devil controls our minds in our dreams it can be a horrifying experience.

(4) We may have nightmares because God is showing us what others, especially people you care about, may be or will be going through. In that case, you will have more understanding of another's pain and have more compassion to help and pray for others.

(5) Sometimes God is showing us what is going to happen in the future so we can pray for protection and be prepared.

(6) We may just be reliving our past painful memories. You need to ask God for healing if you suffer from nightmares related to painful memories.

(7) God may be showing us the reality of our spiritual world, so we can turn around and rely on God for protection.

(8) We may have nightmares because of our sinful attitudes and destructive lifestyles. When our lives are a mess and we follow worldly desires of the flesh, we tend to have more nightmares because we open doors for the devil. We need to repent of our sins, start cleaning up our hearts and lives so the Holy Spirit can help us win our spiritual battles when we are awake or asleep.

(9) When we try to work for God, the devil may attempt to discourage us from doing good through our dreams. We can be attacked even when we are filled with good intentions and good deeds. The devil will try to distract us with worries and fears to keep us from following the Lord. When that happens, it's time to read the Bible and start praying more. Be strong in the Lord and rebuke the devil in Jesus' name to leave you.

7. <u>What are the meanings of dreams?</u> — I believe each dream has meaning and we need to understand that they are not all telling us the future. Some are symbolic, and even the people we see may not be the same person in reality. We need to listen to God to have a clear understanding of what the dream means and what He is trying to tell us. Daniel asked God for dream interpretations, and his prayer was answered. We can follow his example and ask God for interpretation.

8. <u>Is the dream something I am causing?</u> — I have not found any Scripture passages that say we can initiate our own dreams. Some dreams display our habits and lifestyles, but that doesn't mean that we have caused them. God can speak to us while we are asleep through dreams, as well as initiate our dreams. Sometimes Satan will attack us in our dreams which shows that Satan can also initiate dreams.

9. <u>Why do I not remember my dreams on the street, but I come in here (jail) and dream of things I have not thought about in years?</u> — When people are seeking God and have more time to reflect

and pray, their hearts seem to be open to God and they tend to have more dreams. The Lord may want you to take care of things that you have been ignoring for quite some time. Dreams can help us remember things that we have been ignoring.

10. Why can't we remember some of our dreams? — There may be many reasons for this: 1) Some people have a photographic memory of what they dream and some don't. I think it depends on how our brain works and on our ability to remember; 2) Our brain is selective about what we want to remember because we can only hold so much information. Maybe our brain can only remember what seems to be important to us since not all dreams are from the Lord or have spiritual meaning. However, dreams can be useful for reflection and to see where we are mentally, emotionally and spiritually; 3) Sometimes it may be related to what God wants us to remember. There are times we may forget about a certain dream, but the Holy Spirit can help us to remember so we can get a message from the Lord. I am forgetful so I write down my dreams as soon as I wake up. Then, I ask God for understanding so I can pay more attention to what He is trying to tell me.

11. How do we know which dreams are good or bad? — God can help us have peaceful dreams but not all dreams are peaceful even if they come from the Lord. There may be some dreams that forecast future trouble or God may be showing us what is happening in our spiritual walk, not only with the Lord but also with the devil. It's hard for me to label which dreams are good or bad. As long as we listen to God for understanding, there is a lesson from any dream we might have.

12. I dreamt about tornados hitting my old home with my kids in it. What does that mean? — God may be telling you that you need to pray because there is a chance that your family is going through a difficult time or difficult times may be coming up and God is warning you.

13. Why do we have dreams of anger and about hurting people? — Our character, personality and experiences in life can affect our responses in our dreams. Anger and hurting others show that you might have a violent temper that you need to change. Your dream may be telling you that you are harboring resentment. You need

to forgive and take care of your spirit of anger. If we do not take care of our hate and anger, we may act upon those feelings. Your dream may be telling you that this could happen in the future. In that case, God may be warning you to forgive. Ask God to fill your heart with love and to take away your hate and anger. Start praying for people that hurt you. Blessing your enemies will help you forgive.

14. What does it mean when you dream you are going to get high on the outside? — Many who are struggling with addiction to drugs and alcohol have these kinds of dreams. This may be because you still have not let go of your old habits, or you are just experiencing your past. You may be thinking about using drugs or making plans to use drugs when you get out. God may be warning you to quit drinking alcohol and using drugs.

15. I dreamed about being a musician and that is my passion in life. Does that mean God is trying to tell me to go for my dream in life? — Our dreams can be a reflection of what could happen in the future. If your passion is music, God gave you that desire to use your gift. God understands your passion and may be asking you to pursue it or He is showing you what is going to happen in the future. Sometimes our dreams are affected by our past memories, so your mind may be replaying your past.

16. Why do I keep dreaming of my dead relatives? — Your mind may be playing your past memories. If your deceased relatives were Christians, their presence in your dreams may have a message that you need to know. I believe when people die, they go to heaven if they believed in God. If they did not believe in God they go to hell. I do not believe there are dead spirits wandering around. The devil can disguise himself as a deceased family member or other dead people to appeal to us. You need to ask God why you are seeing them.

17. Does the Lord give messages to us through dreams? — Yes, if that dream is initiated by God. However, all of our dreams can have a message about our spiritual condition, even though it may be caused by some reason other than God. We need God's wisdom to understand it.

18. When you dream, can you wake up and have marks on you? Or what is that when you wake up with cuts deep in your skin? —

There could be many reasons. You may have hurt yourself while sleeping. If you have no recollection of hurting yourself, there may be a spirit hurting you while you are asleep. I have never seen or met anyone who had this problem. You need to pray for protection if you feel you are being attacked by the devil. Start reading the Bible and pray more to be strong in the Lord. You do not have to be afraid of the devil.

19. Are there dreams from God and from Satan? — The spiritual world is real, therefore, some dreams can be from God and some can be from Satan. If we are walking with God, we will have less chance of being attacked by the devil in dreams. Though even strong Christians can be attacked by the devil. The devil will run away when you are spiritually strong in your walk with God, even in your dream. Jesus gives us power to overcome the enemy, and this applies not only when we are awake, but also while we sleep.

20. What does God want us to know through dreams? — He wants to teach us many things, especially how to listen and develop an intimate relationship with Him. God created us so we can have a close relationship with Him. There is no relationship when we do not know the person. God wants us to know His power and love by helping us to know what is happening and what is going to happen. We can speak to Him through prayer, but just talking to Him is one-way communication. Until you learn to listen, you cannot develop a close relationship with Him. God speaks to us through the Word of God and through dreams. The Holy Spirit speaks to our minds and hearts to guide, teach, and direct us. Our faith will grow when we pay attention to dreams and learn to listen to God's voice.

21. How do we know which dreams are from God? — If a dream has some spiritual meaning or discernable message for our benefit, I believe it came from God. We can learn from all dreams, and we can ask God what a dream means, even though we may have been attacked spiritually in it.

22. Is there a person out there like Daniel? — God has so much more power than we think or imagine. He blesses people who are open to listening to Him with His wisdom, knowledge, understanding, power, and insight. I believe God speaks to people even now and

helps them interpret dreams. So, yes, I believe there are people like Daniel.

23. <u>Why do people have violent dreams while incarcerated</u>? — Many incarcerated people are hurting and vulnerable, and the devil uses this opportunity to attack. If you have grown up in a violent home or experienced violence in your life, there is a chance that you may relive it. You need to pray for peace and start reading the Bible. The Word of God has spiritual power. Read *1 Peter 5:6-11* and *Ephesians 6:10-20* to understand spiritual battle. Also, pray so you can be spiritually strong to handle the attacks.

24. <u>When demons attack you in your dream, when you wake up, why do you feel that attack</u>? — Satan's attack is real to those whose spiritual senses are open to spiritual reality, whether they are awake or asleep. We need to be strong in order to defend ourselves in our dreams. It's important to read the Bible because the Word of God can equip us to win the spiritual battle. Spend time in prayer for commitment and obey the Lord when He asks you to do something. The devil has less power over us if we focus our hearts on God and try to live godly lives. We can rebuke the devil when we feel the devil's attacks, whether we are awake or asleep. We have the power to overcome the enemy in Jesus' name and with the power of His blood. If we do not have a relationship with Jesus, there is no protection. Spiritual knowledge, power, and authority do not come from just knowing the Bible, but by developing a close relationship with the Lord and by obeying Him and learning to resist the devil.

25. <u>Why do I have such evil dreams about sinful things that God doesn't want me to be doing? I'm coming off of heroin and I am still having recurring dreams about using and some of the dreams are violent and sexually oriented</u>. — We are all in the process of cleaning our spiritual houses. Some have a difficult time letting go of their bad habits. Until we are determined to obey the Lord, the dream is showing us that we still have the chance of falling into sin. We should have the determination to resist sin, even in our dreams. This takes spiritual discipline and an obedient heart.

26. <u>What does it mean when we die in our dreams? Is it a spiritual warning that we are on the wrong path</u>? — It may mean many things. We may be dying for worldly desires, or God may be

warning us to prepare for our meeting with the Lord. You might be heading toward some trouble and you need to pray. If you can listen to God's voice for interpretation of the dream, you can find peace because He will reveal things to you.

27. <u>Do our dreams about Jesus or the Lord have real meaning in our lives?</u> — I believe when people see Jesus in their dreams it's a blessing because we can have a deeper understanding of who Jesus is. Many times people understand why Jesus came to them. If you do not know why you saw Jesus in your dream, you can ask God why or what He is trying to tell you.

28. <u>Do dreams tell us about the future? Do dreams actually come true?</u> — It depends on whether God is telling you about your future or not. That's why it is important to recognize His voice.

29. <u>Why do I dream about demons that get into people and I am the one who saves them? I pray to God that demons come out.</u> — This dream may be telling you that you are strong in the Lord and your prayer is helping others, or God may be encouraging you to pray more for others. Ask God what it means.

30. <u>Why do I dream of friends I have not seen in a long time? When they come after me they try to hurt me as if to kill me, and I cannot get away. I wake up in a cold sweat. Why is that?</u> — I believe this friend in your dream is not your friend. It is the devil appearing to you in the form of your friend. Maybe God is warning you that you will have problems with this person, and you need to pray for wisdom. When you neglect reading the Bible and are not praying, you are opening the door for the devil. Read the Bible, pray, repent, change your lifestyle, so you can live a pure and holy life. Ask God to help you so you can have peaceful dreams. You also can rebuke the devil in your dreams, in Jesus' name. If there are things you need to take care of, try to do it so you will be spiritually healthy. Remember, even strong Christians can have bad dreams. Do not be alarmed, but keep praying and asking God for understanding.

31. <u>How do we know when a good or bad spirit is talking to us in a dream?</u> — If you have a gift of discernment, you will know which spirit is talking to you. You might need to pray to God to give you understanding. Usually, bad spirits are evil spirits who like to hurt and torture us. A good spirit, in my understanding, is

any spirit that is on God's side, such as angels or other Christians who are walking with the Holy Spirit.

32. How do we know when the Holy Spirit interprets a dream for us? — If you are aware of how the Holy Spirit speaks to you, you will know whether or not your dream interpretation came from the Lord. If you have not learned to recognize His voice, you can evaluate to see if you heard Him by reflecting on the following question: Did you ask the Holy Spirit for interpretation of your dream? If an understanding came after you prayed and you knew that there was no way you could have invented that understanding and the Word of God agrees with the voice you have heard, then I believe the Holy Spirit has helped you interpret the dream. Sometimes what God tells you might not make sense, but wait and see if you heard him right by reflecting on this matter later. If you are not familiar with the Holy Spirit's voice, I encourage you to practice listening in prayer, in silence. Be aware that the devil can also speak to your mind to distract you.

33. Why is the devil always trying to attack me in my sleep? — When you are sleeping, you are at rest and potentially more receptive to suggestions and images. You need the gifts of discernment, and to be strong in the Lord so you can guard yourself. Read *Ephesians 6:10-20* to find out which area you need to strengthen. When you are strong in the Lord and obeying Him, you will be strong even in your dreams.

34. Why do I dream about fire? — In my spiritual journey, fire is a good thing, especially when I spend lots of time in prayer. It signifies the Holy Spirit's purifying fire through prayer and cleansing of a heart. But if someone experiences the fires of hell in their dream, fire may not be considered as purification but torture and warning.

35. Why am I always being hurt in my dreams? — In reality, you may be hurting spiritually or emotionally and you need healing. Start reading the Bible, pray to be strong and leave all kinds of sin, so you can win the spiritual battle. Also, ask the Lord to heal your wounds and rebuke the devil in Jesus' name to leave you. If you are holding resentment against anyone, forgive them. When

you do not forgive, you are inviting the spirit of resentment and torment, and it may be showing in your dreams.

36. <u>When I close my eyes, I see vivid presences such as Jesus, God's divine Spirit, or people that wish to be in my presence. What does that mean?</u> — You may not be dreaming. God may be giving you spiritual visions in your mind to understand Jesus better. Ask God why you have these spiritual visions. The Holy Spirit can give you spiritual visions in your mind. When the same vision keeps coming to you, ask God why you are seeing the vision.

37. <u>I have dreams of living in a beautiful and colorful place but I have not been able to find it</u>. — God may have given you the dream to see and experience this spiritual heavenly place. You have felt and seen the beauty in spirit. Our spiritual senses are much deeper than our physical senses.

Part Three:
Reflections and Dreams

Chaplain McDonald

1. Dreams can help us to hear God's voice.

In 1996, when God first called me to ministry, I was running away from the Lord like Jonah. About a year later, I felt I only should spend ten percent of my time in prayer every day, somewhat like tithing. I dismissed it at first because my prayer wouldn't even last five minutes in those days. When this thought of praying persisted, I concluded that the Holy Spirit was asking it of me. Even though I didn't want to go into the ministry, I thought at least I should try to pray. In 1997, I started going to church early in the mornings and spending time with God in prayer.

After I spent more time with God in prayer, I started having many dreams. I knew these dreams had spiritual meaning but I could not understand them.

During this time, God sent Frank and Patty Lambert into my life. They became my spiritual mentors. They were both ministers who reach out to Native Americans. One day I shared my dreams with Patty and asked her if she could tell me the meaning of the dreams. Occasionally Patty would share her thoughts. One day she asked me if I had asked God for help. I replied, "No." She said, "Ask God for the interpretations of your dreams. He will tell you what they mean."

No one had told me to ask God for interpretations before. In fact, I was skeptical at first. I was not sure whether or not God would help me understand. I asked myself, "How will I be able to hear God's voice?" However, I followed Patty's suggestion. Whenever I had a dream I wrote it down and asked, "God, what are you trying to say to me? Please help me to understand it." I waited in silence then wrote down the words that came to my heart. The results were remarkable. Through this practice, I learned to listen to God's voice. He not only gave me interpretations, but also spoke to me about other things as well. My relationship with the Lord grew, and I haven't been the same since. Patty's suggestion helped me to initiate conversations with God. This changed my walk with the Lord.

After gaining confidence that God would answer me, I started asking more questions. Whenever I could not understand what was happening in my spiritual walk, I would ask God and He started sharing His heart. I have confidence that the Holy Spirit is ready to give me answers when I need them. I am forever thankful for Patty's suggestion.

2. Dreams can help us understand what is happening and what is going to happen in the future.

While I was growing up, I learned that God spoke to my mother through dreams. She never taught me how to listen to God or told me I should pay attention to my dreams. Nevertheless, she did teach me that through dreams God can reveal things to people. My mother occasionally asked me questions because she had dreams about me. She knew what was going on in my life. Because of this, I learned that there was nothing I could really hide from her.

God spoke to me about my children and my family's spiritual conditions through dreams, especially concerning critical events. God has given me these dreams so I can pray for my children and understand what they are going through to be able to encourage them. It has given me so much comfort knowing that God cares about me enough to share what is going to happen through my dreams.

3. Dreams can teach us about our spiritual conditions and the spiritual world.

On many occasions, God has spoken to me about my spiritual condition through dreams. If I am walking with God, reading the Bible, praying, and working to do the right thing by obeying the Holy Spirit's leading, then I am strong. When I see the devil in my dreams, I rebuke him in the name of Jesus and win the battle. The devil cannot hurt me when I am walking with the Lord. If I do not obey or lose focus on Jesus or walk in the path of sin, the devil is strong not only while I am awake but also in my dreams.

I have also learned that even when I am working hard to obey the Lord, the devil will try to scare me. During these times I've learned that the best thing to do is to rebuke the devil in Jesus' name, keep studying the Word of God, and pray to be strong in the Lord. Nightmares reflect that we need to be stronger in the Lord through prayer and that we need to rely on God's Word to win these battles.

To follow Jesus, we need to be transformed in our minds and hearts so we will be able to think the way God wants us to. If we are not transformed in our thoughts and behaviors, our old sinful selves and the devil will lead us onto a destructive path and we may not even realize it.

My dreams have given me more confidence, assuring me that God is stronger than the devil. When the devil tries to plant the seed of fear and doubt, I keep proclaiming victory in God's name. When people learn to fight the devil with the Word of God, they can have peace. *(John 14:27)*

Paul teaches us about the spiritual battle. *"Finally, be strong in the Lord and in his mighty power. Put on the full armor of God so that you can take your stand against the devil's schemes. For our struggle is not against flesh and blood, but against the rulers, against the authorities, against the powers of this dark world and against the spiritual forces of evil in the heavenly realms. Therefore put on the full armor of God, so that when the day of evil comes, you may be able to stand your ground, and after you have done everything, to stand. Stand firm then, with the belt of truth buckled around your waist, with the breastplate of righteousness in place, and with your feet fitted with the readiness that comes from the gospel of peace. In addition to all this, take up the shield of faith, with which you can extinguish all the flaming arrows of the evil one. Take the helmet of salvation and the sword of the Spirit, which is the Word of God. And pray in the Spirit on all occasions with all kinds of prayers and requests. With this in mind, be alert and always keep on praying for all the saints."* (Ephesians 6:10-18)

James also warns how to deal with the devil. *"But he gives us more grace. That is why Scripture says: 'God opposes the proud but gives grace to the humble.' Submit yourselves, then, to God. Resist the devil, and he will flee from you."* (James 4:6-7)

Our victory comes when we grow in love for the Lord and obey Him by resisting and leaving sinful thoughts and behaviors. Prayer is a great spiritual weapon against the devil's lies. The Word of God gives us direction on how to win the battle. Without prayer, we cannot experience victory over the devil's attacks.

4. Some dreams are gifts from the Holy Spirit.

Not everyone dreams and not everyone is gifted with dreams. One example of how the Holy Spirit blesses God's children is through dreams. Joel talked about dreams being one of the signs of the outpouring of the Holy Spirit. When Peter was filled with the Holy Spirit, he recited what Joel had written: *"In the last days, God says, I will pour out my Spirit on all people. Your sons and daughters will prophesy. Your young men will see visions. Your old men will dream dreams. Even on my servants, both men and women, I will pour out my Spirit on those days. And they will prophesy." (Acts 2:17 -18)*

Jesus said that the Holy Spirit will guide, direct, comfort, and teach us about the future. The Holy Spirit has guided me in dreams in my everyday life and regarding which church I should attend. Jesus said, *"But the Counselor, the Holy Spirit, whom the Father will send in my name, will teach you all things and will remind you of everything I have said to you." (John 14:26) "And I will ask the Father, and he will give you another counselor to be with you forever --the Spirit of truth. The world cannot accept him, because it neither sees him nor knows him. But you know him, for he lives with you and will be in you." (John 14:16-17)* Our close relationship with the Holy Spirit is key to understanding our dreams. Those who ask shall receive, and the Holy Spirit is willing to speak to us if we spend time waiting and searching.

In addition, I believe the devil can initiate dreams to torment people. We need to read the Word of God, pray, and obey the Lord to be strong and leave our life of sin, so that we do not open doors for the devil to come in and torture us.

5. Some dreams are gifts from God to help each other.

Some dreams may tell us about other people's spiritual conditions while others may tell what is going to happen to them or how they will affect my spiritual journey. Some dreams are more or less symbolic. For example, the people I see in some of my dreams are not always the same people portrayed in real life. When I ask God, He helps me to understand who the person is. Without the Holy Spirit revealing it to me, I wouldn't know. I am learning how important it is to rely on God to understand when to share, what to share, and with whom. *"Listen to my words: 'When a prophet of the Lord is among you, I reveal myself to him in visions, I speak to him in dreams.'" (Numbers 12:6)*

6. Be persistent in prayer to receive understanding of dreams.

Understanding God's voice takes time and patience, but it's always worth it. We must be persistent if we want to sharpen our spiritual senses for understanding and conviction. He speaks to us in many different ways with or without words. Sometimes God gives us wisdom and knowledge that go beyond our human understanding. If we are not listening, we might miss the gentle, small voice of the Holy Spirit in our hearts. Moreover, we have to learn to be patient before God. Many people give up too early on a response. It is important to keep asking God until understanding comes. You will know when He has answered you.

To those who are having a difficult time recognizing where the voices are coming from, quiet your mind and try to listen to God in silence and examine your thoughts. The voices can come from any or all of these four sources: the devil, the Holy Spirit, other people and yourself. Examine whatever thoughts come to your mind to figure out their origin. If it comes from the devil, it will be either impure, judgmental, critical, earthly, selfish, or destructive. *(James 2:14-16)* If it comes from the Holy Spirit, it can create peace and all the good things that will help us to grow in faith. The Holy Spirit will give you wise suggestions on how to grow in a loving relationship with the Lord and how to help others grow in faith. There are thoughts which come from other people's voices and worldly concepts. Also, you have your own voice. You have the final decision which voice you will accept and which one you will discard. Recognize which is your flesh or sinful talk and which is your newborn spirit's voice. With so many voices, you may be confused at first, but as you reflect and examine the Scriptures, you will know which voice you need to follow. The Scripture tells us, *"Be still before the Lord and wait patiently for him." (Psalm 37:7)*

This practice of waiting and listening in silence will open your spiritual senses and help you understand God's interpretations of your dreams. Instead of talking all the time in prayer, practice listening more in your prayers. Listening to His voice will revolutionize your spiritual growth. I count the days when I pray, asking God for an answer in silence. My patience pays off when God speaks to me and gives me answers "no," or "yes," or other insights. God lets me know when to change my prayers.

I have a Christian friend who spends a lot of time in prayer. One day, she shared concerns she was having about her dreams. I believed God was trying to tell her something. She told me that even after she had asked Him, understanding did not come. I told her not to be discouraged, but to keep asking. Later on she told me about how understanding had finally come when she was least expecting it. She had no doubt that the Lord was answering her prayers.

7. How to understand your dream in light of the Scriptures.

I encourage everyone who reads this book to spend time reading the Bible and to see how people in the Bible came to understand their dreams. Ask the Holy Spirit to give you wisdom, knowledge, understanding and revelation to understand your dreams. Learn to wait before God and let go of disruptions and distractions, so you can understand what God is trying to tell you. Remember, if anything opposes the Scriptures, question it. When you are in doubt, keep asking God for clarification, and then wait. In this way, you will learn to recognize the voice of the Holy Spirit.

8. You can learn more about dreams through the Bible.

The following Bible verses are biblical references that talk about dreams and interpretations. You can read them and learn more about how God speaks to people and how He helped them to understand their dreams and dreams of others.

Genesis: 20:3,6; 28:12; 31:10,11,24; 37:5,6,8,9,10; 40:5,8,9,16,22; 41:1,5,7,8,11,12,15,17,22,25,26,32; 42:9
Numbers: 20:6
Deuteronomy: 13:1
Judges: 7:13,15
1 Samuel: 28:6, 15
1 Kings: 3:5,15

Job: 4:13; 7:14; 20:8; 33:15
Psalm: 73:20; 126:1
Ecclesiastes: 5:3
Isaiah: 29:7,8; 56:10
Jeremiah: 23:25,27,28,32; 27:9; 29:8
Daniel: 1:17; 2:1,2,3,4,5,6,7,9,16,23,24,25,26,28,36,45; 2:45;
4:5,6,7,8,9,18,19,24; 5:12; 7:1,16
Joel: 2:28
Zechariah: 10:2
Matthew: 1:20; 2:12,13,19,22; 27:19
Acts: 2:17

Part Four:
Dreams and Interpretations

Chaplain McDonald

My understanding of dreams is the result of God's grace through answers to my prayers. I will share how God has blessed me with dreams and how He has helped me in my spiritual journey.

1. Dreams before I came to America

1) Snakes
During my early teen years, I had a terrifying dream about snakes. There were many huge, shining snakes in my parents' bedroom. The snakes were bright orange, red, blue, and yellow. They were making big circles. They were so big that they filled the whole room. They were not ordinary snakes.

After I woke up, I could not understand why I had this dream. My parents started to have marital problems around this time. My father started drinking more and became physically abusive toward my older brother and mother. My older brother ran away from home. Also, my father openly said things against the church and hated his family for attending church. Life became unbearably difficult because of my parents' fights. My family lived in fear because my father's abusive behaviors. Throughout this dream, I believe God was trying to tell me that my parents' marital problems were more than what they appeared to be; it was a spiritual battle. My father did not recognize it, but I believe he was influenced by the devil who was trying to make his entire family quit going to church. During this time there was no law prohibiting my father's abusive behavior, so no one was able to stop him. The devil used my father to hurt his family.

2) A Friend
I always had faith in God but I backslid during my teenage years. My father was against Christianity during this time. I did not want any conflict with him, so I stopped attending church. I started

spending time with non-Christian friends. One of my friends committed suicide. After I saw her dead body, I started having nightmares.

In this dream, she came over to our house and clung to me. In terror, I would scream and try to push her away, but she was too strong. Then my mother would appear and tell her to leave. The girl cried bitterly and then left. At the end of the dream something was choking me, so I called to God for help to free me. I was terrified to go to sleep because of these nightmares; I also suffered from headaches. My mother would put her hands on my forehead and pray, then the headaches would immediately disappear. God answered her prayers and I started to realize that God was real. During this time my eyesight was getting bad. My mother told me to go back to church, so I did. My eyesight got better plus the nightmares disappeared soon after that. I experienced God's healing power through my mother's prayer.

I believe these dreams about my friend indicate that the devil was attacking me because I did not have much faith in God. I am glad my mother was able to help me out of this situation. She has been my spiritual mentor and has taught me about spiritual warfare more than anyone else I have ever met.

3) My Sister

After my younger sister, only 18 years old, died in a car accident, she came to see me in a dream. I told her I thought she was dead. She smiled at me and said that she did not die. After that, something was choking my neck. Many times when I had dreams about her, they were nightmares and someone was trying to choke me. I could not breathe, so I would call on God to help me. I had a difficult time waking up from these dreams.

I was terrified to go to sleep and suffered more headaches. I was depressed that I was not able to do anything. I had no idea what was happening to me. I had no knowledge of spiritual battles at the time. I did not realize that prayer and my relationship with God would help me win my spiritual battle. Because of that, in my critical times, the devil attacked me. I was tormented with nightmares.

Before I started having these nightmares, I used to spent a lot of time listening to worldly pop music and reading philosophical and psychological books. Since I started having nightmares, I could not listen to pop music or read books because I would get headaches. During this time, I was attending church but my perception of the world was gloomy. I had no idea that God had plans for my life through Christ. I was professing to be a Christian but I was not following the Lord's way. I had no idea how to commit my life to the Lord. I was living in sin and I did not even realize it.

The devil was hurting me in my dreams and that's what was happening in my real world as well. I did not know that a sinful lifestyle allowed the devil to hurt me. My worldly thoughts and actions did not glorify God. Accepting the thoughts of despair and hopelessness hurt me. I was relying on human understanding of life not the Word of God. Being raised in a culture that does not value girls did not help me. I suffered from inferior feelings, and my heart was filled with fear and worries.

My Mother gave me the best advice during this critical time. She said, "Read the Bible." Until then I only carried the Bible to church. This time I understood the Bible for the first time. When I could not read any other books, I was able to read the Bible which had spiritual power. I started reading Romans and was suddenly convinced that I was a sinner. I used to think that I was a good person, but while reading the Scriptures I started to understand that I was a terrible sinner. I asked God to forgive me. For the first time in my life, I had peace of mind. I experienced God's forgiveness. I loved studying the Bible so much, that I attended the Suwon Bible College.

While I was attending school, God opened my eyes to the spiritual world. When I looked at certain people, I could see that they were influenced by the devil. It was scary for me. I knew that if I did not rely on Jesus, the devil would try to hurt me. Also, when I would begin to read other books, before I even read a full page, I was able to sense the authors' spiritual condition. If they were influenced by worldly knowledge, I could tell and reading it would give me a headache.

I learned about how our mind is a spiritual battlefield through Watchman Lee's *Spiritual Man*. This book helped me more than any other book besides the Bible. Through this book, I learned how to use the Word of God to fight the negative, accusing voices of the devil. I did not realize that negative thoughts could be planted by the devil. Moreover, our spiritual condition affects our dreams. My dreams were reflections of what was happening in the spiritual world around me. My mother assured me that my sister was in heaven and asked me to fight the devil in Jesus' name. This helped me tremendously. Eventually, I was delivered from nightmares and depression with help from God, the Bible and prayer.

4) My Father

One Summer, my father went on a prayer retreat with my mother. Prior to this, my father would fight with her whenever she would decide to go on a retreat. I did not have much hope for my father. The night before my father came home I had a dream. I saw my father's face and it was bright.

When I woke up from my dream, I knew that my father had met God. My father came home changed. He started attending church and decided not to drink or smoke. Unfortunately, this only lasted about three months before he reverted back to his old lifestyle.

2. Dreams before I responded to my call to ministry

5) A Heavenly Room

While my husband was pastor in Plains, Montana, I had a dream in which I died. I was going up to heaven with only a single regret. I had wanted to help my mother financially but had not been able to do so. When I went up to heaven an angel took me to a room which had been set aside for me. I was disappointed that my room was so small. The angel told me that I did not do much work for God while I was living on earth so my room was small.

I had not taken Jesus' word literally but he spoke about preparing rooms for His disciples. At the time I was backsliding and complained to God and whomever else would listen about how much I disliked being a pastor's wife. I think God was trying to encourage me to work for His kingdom, but I ignored Him. I reached a point when I started doubting God's existence. I could not figure out how I had lost my faith. God questioned me to find out how I had lost my first love. As I reflect, when I stopped reading the Bible, I lost faith in God. After I started reading it, I found God.

6) Two Churches

After my husband had been the pastor at the Glasgow and Hinsdale churches for about two years, I had this dream. I was looking down on the Hinsdale church where two dogs were running in circles. The people started following the dogs, making two big circles. My husband was pushed out of the pulpit and was standing by the door. Although my husband did not have any problems with the Hinsdale congregation his first year, he did have a difficult time the second year. I did not pay much attention to this because I was attending only Glasgow church, and not Hinsdale. The dream convinced me that more trouble was coming. Within a week, my husband got a phone call from his district superintendent telling him that a person from Hinsdale had written a letter intending to hurt him. This had never happened to him before.

The district superintendent came out to have a special conflict meeting. I was so disgusted with the whole situation that I told him I was not going. He told me that there might be something I could learn, so I went. When I walked into the basement where they were having the meeting, I felt the devil's attack. I learned that some people have the gift of spiritual discernment and sometimes God lets me understand what is happening in the spiritual realm. The only way I could fight this was by praying to God and rebuking the devil. This is why I believe that spiritual warfare is real. From this early experience, I learned that what my husband was going through was spiritual conflict. If the devil could stir up the church through conflict by accusing their spiritual leader, there would be less room for reaching out to the lost people. After this, I spent lots of time praying for Hinsdale.

7) The Basement

I had a dream I was renting out a basement to an old woman. The basement was filled with antiques and beautiful decorations, but the woman would not clean. Every room was filled with garbage. The lady did not even pick up her mail which other people had brought her. My daughter and I started cleaning. There were many rooms and we became tired. One room had a newborn baby which still had the umbilical cord attached. I told the woman that I would not clean any more because it was her responsibility.

I asked God about the meaning of the dream. God spoke to my heart, telling me that the basement I was cleaning represented the situation in the Hinsdale church. I understood then that the rooms I had been cleaning in my dream represented my prayers for other people's hearts to be clean. Three days after I had this dream, the district superintendent came out and told my husband that another pastor would be sent out to the Hinsdale church.

8) Cleaning

One day, I had a dream about the Glasgow church. There was a room in the church that was filled with garbage. My daughter and my son were with me cleaning. When we finished cleaning, I saw a big crack in the floor. Then someone told me the name of the person who was responsible.

I could not understand what the meaning of the dream was. Three days after I had this dream, I realized that I was having a problem with the person who was responsible for cleaning this one room in the church. I prayed a lot for this person and God helped me to forgive that individual.

9) Digging

I was standing in the Glasgow sanctuary with my daughter in a dream. The floor of the sanctuary was dirt. I saw a dog digging a hole in the floor. I was alarmed but did not know how to stop the dog.

Because of my previous dreams about dogs, I recognized that they were an indication of a problem. I asked God who that person was. God gave me the name. I told my husband about my dream and asked him to be careful with this person, but he did not pay any attention to me. About three months later, he had problems with this person in the sanctuary. My husband never had anything like this happen to him before while he was in ministry.

10) A House

I had a dream that I was visiting Frank and Patty Lambert's house which was built on the top of the river. I knew the couple very well. Frank and Patty were good friends of mine and devoted Native American missionaries. I was inside their home. The whole house was made out of clear glass; it was the most beautiful thing I had ever seen. I could feel the beauty of the house and the river. Somehow I knew that the river was the Holy Spirit.

After I had this dream, I gained more respect for Patty and Frank who have a heart for ministry. They were my spiritual mentors while I was living in Glasgow. Patty was the one who told me to ask God for the interpretation of dreams, and that advice has helped my spiritual growth. I believe God gave me this dream to show me just how deeply committed they were to God's work and how sensitive they were to the Holy Spirit's leading. I had this dream in the middle of the week, and the following Sunday they came to visit our church in Glasgow for the first time. They asked us if the Glasgow church could host a Native American Christmas dinner. I organized it, the church prepared the food, and Frank and Patty prepared wonderful gifts. Many people came, and it was a great success!

11) A Voice

During a time when God had put it on my heart to fast for three days in Glasgow, I had a hard time getting motivated. It took a long time to commit myself to doing this. The last time I had fasted was when I was trying to decide if marrying my husband was what God wanted. God did not say no, so I took it as a yes and got married. I never doubted that my husband was the answer to my prayer. This time, there was no particular reason, except for feeling that God wanted me to fast. I figured that God must have something to teach me.

I had a dream the night before I began fasting. I was holding a round wooden frame which had threads of wool like cobwebs across it, and there were many fishhooks tangled in the middle of it. My responsibility was to remove all of the hooks, one by one. While I was working at it, I heard a demonic voice right behind me. I knew it was the devil trying to stop me but I kept on working.

This was the first time that I had heard a demonic voice in my dreams. I woke up wondering why I had this dream. During the first day of the fast, my family had many arguments, everyone was irritable, and my husband told me I should stop fasting. I remembered the dream and decided I shouldn't quit. I was convinced that God had some lesson to teach me. I believe that our family had not been living godly lives, and God was trying to tell me that we needed to change the way we talked and how we treated each other.

12) Animals

During the three-day fast mentioned above, I had many dreams. In one dream, I was trying to change a clock on the wall. The time was wrong and I was trying to move the numbers. My son was there. I did not see him but could feel his presence. I said to him, "I am having a difficult time changing this clock back to the right time. Do you think you could help me change the time?"

He answered, "No, you cannot go back in time." I tried again to change the clock. Then, suddenly, the numbers on the clock turned into an ugly looking bird, a mouse, and other filthy small animals. I quickly put them in a dustpan and put them outside.

Through this dream, I was convinced God was again telling me that our family was not living holy lives and needed some change. Prayer is a part of cleansing ourselves, and that is what God was teaching me. It is impossible to go back and change our past. Recognizing that we have made some mistakes is important, so we do not make the same ones again.

3. Dreams after I made the commitment to go into the ministry

13) A Visit

Peter appeared in my dream, shook my hand and disappeared.

I had this dream right after I had made the decision to respond to the call to the ministry. I believed this was a confirmation from God saying that I made the right decision. I heard God's voice saying, "Preach, preach," but I did not want to answer this call. God had plans for my life, but I made my own plans, buying many rental houses. When I decided to go into the real-estate business, God spoke to me, "Don't sell houses. Sell God." I didn't go into real-estate because of that and it was a long and painful struggle to let go of my rentals later. Once I finally gave up my plans and decided to go into the ministry, my life was never the same again. It was hard at first but later ministry became a blessing.

14) Prayers

One Sunday morning as I was praying, God spoke to me about Frank who had been suffering from cancer. His wife, Ivy, attended our church but Frank never attended church. He had been sick for a while but I did not visit him because I did not know him very well. I had only met him once, five years before, when Ivy invited my family to Christmas dinner at her restaurant.

I was not praying for Frank that morning but God spoke to me about three things about him: First, Frank's time was short. I understood then that he would not live too long. Second, God gave me the Scripture, *"snatch others from the fire and save them; to others show mercy, mixed with fear--hating even the clothing stained by corrupted flesh." (Jude 1:23)* I understood that I needed to go and share the gospel with him. Third, God gave me words, "He is my son." I understood that somehow God would open his heart and save him.

That morning I met Ivy at the church. I asked her how Frank was doing. She told me he was in the hospital and was not doing well. Ivy told me how much she was concerned about Frank's salvation. She shared that when Frank first got sick, her son wrote him a long letter describing why he should accept Christ before he died so he can be saved. Frank was upset and threw his son's letter away.

I told Ivy I would like to visit Frank. She responded, "No, he doesn't look good." I did not tell her that God asked me to visit him because I was not sure how she would take it. However, I told her that God may have some lessons for me to learn from this visit. She still was reluctant but I was persistent. She finally took me to the hospital but before we arrived there, Ivy told me that Frank was not open to Christianity.

After Ivy introduced me to Frank, I asked him how he was spending time in the hospital. He told me he was praying. I asked, "Have you met Jesus?" He answered, "Yes." I was amazed. "How did you meet him?" He replied, "I was mowing the lawn one day. Jesus came to see me." I asked, "Did Jesus say anything to you?" Frank replied, "He told me to pray." I asked, "What did you tell him?" He said, "I told him I will pray later."

"So, that's why you are praying?" I said. Frank nodded his

head and said, "Yes." I asked Frank if he would like to pray with me, he said, "Yes." Three of us held hands and I prayed for Frank. Many people were praying for Frank and concerned about his salvation. God had opened Frank's heart so he can understand Jesus was real. It was God's grace that Jesus appeared to Frank to tell him to pray.

Three days after I visited Frank, I had a dream. Frank was surrounded with prayers that looked like clouds. Ten percent of the prayers were leaking out of the hole, and I was in a shock and concerned.

I woke up and asked God about the meaning of the dream. The answer came that Frank was dying. Then God spoke to me that my job was done and that I did not need to visit Frank any more. Ivy could not understand why I wouldn't go and visit Frank, but I told her that God was telling me I did not need to. I gave her a tape of hymns to play for him. The following Monday, I visited Frank with my husband and asked him if we could sing hymns for him and he said, "Yes." We sang many hymns for him, then he thanked us.

The next morning Frank died. After Frank died, I wondered if he was saved. Then 25 days after Frank passed away, God gave me a dream. Frank came to see me. He shook my hand and said, "I am going on a long journey and came to say good-bye to you." Right behind him I saw a long narrow road stretching up all the way to heaven. An unfamiliar man was standing behind him.

When I woke up, I asked God who the other man was. The answer came to my heart. He was Frank's guardian angel. I was convinced Frank was saved. I believe God gave me that dream, so I did not have to question his salvation. Later I shared this dream with Ivy. After her husband died, she called me and told me she was wondering if Frank was saved. I had no doubt that he was saved because of this dream. It was a confirmation from the Lord that Frank was saved, which comforted Ivy.

15) A Barn

In a dream I saw an old, shabby, ugly-looking barn that had to be torn down. I was the only person there, and in my right hand, I was holding three pieces of wood which came from the barn. It seemed I was the owner.

I asked God the meaning of the dream, and He said, "My

daughter, you are harvesting resentment against your husband. I already told you that I am the one who will help you go to school, not him. Forgive him."

After I made a decision to go into the ministry, I expected that my husband would be happy about my decision to serve God. To my surprise, he was not. He wanted a wife who would support him, and he wanted to live in a small town in Montana. He did not want to move. The closest United Methodist Seminary was in Denver. Since I could not convince him to move, I decided to commute. I was disappointed and resented the fact that he would not support my decision. I had supported him when he attended seminary. I expected that he would do the same. I was wrong and was so upset that I cried for two days. That's when I had this dream.

That morning, I said to my husband, "I've decided not to fight with you any more, and I forgive you." From that experience, I learned that I should not expect anything from my husband. From time to time, God has helped me to realize how much I am blessed because of my husband's love and faithfulness.

16) A Fight

After I made the decision to go into the ministry, I decided to cut out worldly entertainment in order to focus on my spiritual growth. This was not a difficult decision, because I did not like watching television or have any hobbies other than reading Christian books. I decided to read the gospels and concentrate on prayer and meditation to help me better understand Jesus.

One day I was so upset that I did not read the Bible. That evening, I had a dream that a group of men walked into our home. One of them was a strong man with mud on his shoes. He stood on the couch and started rubbing his dirty shoes against it. I told them to get out. The man on the couch grabbed my hands and I struggled with him. He was too strong and I was weak. When I woke up, I knew what the problem was. The rough people represented evil spirits. The Word of God is our source of spiritual strength and power. I let the devil win by intentionally not reading the Bible. Since that dream, no matter what other people do to me, I keep my heart focused on God by reading the Bible. The devil was trying to discourage me by distracting me from reading the Bible. I lost peace and opened myself to the devil's attack.

Another time when I was discouraged and had neglected reading the Bible, I had yet another dream. I was going down a hill on a slippery dirt road that was covered with many little snakes. I quickly turned around, went back up the hill and left. From these dreams, I learned that the spiritual battle is always there. The Word of God has spiritual power to help me.

17) A Helper

I dreamt I heard a loud voice warning me to hide. A man appeared and told me to hide and to avoid evil people. I bent down by a window and saw a group of men walking by. They seemed to want to hurt people. Suddenly, it was winter and I was going on a hurried journey by myself. I was holding a blanket in case I needed it. I was walking, but I was going up and down a steep hill so fast it seemed as though I was driving. The blanket was heavy and was slowing me down. When I was on top of the hill, the man reappeared and told another man to come and help me. I gave the blanket to the man who was ready to help me and said, "This is not a new blanket. I don't need it any more. Please wash it, and give it to someone else who can use it." Then the man reappeared a third time. He told another man to provide a pair of shoes for me. I had not even realized that I was barefoot. The first pair of shoes were made of cloth material which would not be good for a long journey in the winter. Not long after I started walking, some other people came and gave me leather boots. As I walked a bit more, someone gave me a warm coat. I suddenly realized I had everything I needed.

When I woke up from that dream, I understood that the man who was helping me was the Holy Sprit. This dream gave me comfort. My understanding is that the blanket I was carrying was the rental business that I had. When I decided to go into the ministry, God spoke to my heart telling me that I needed to sell all of my rentals, including the house we lived in Glasgow, for they had become a burden. I now understood why God had asked me to sell them.

The fast journey represented our sudden move to Buffalo, Wyoming, which was closer to the seminary, and the ministry that God was going to lead me into just as soon as I started school. The shoes, I believe, indicated how God was going to take care of me and how He would direct my future ministry.

I asked the Lord about what the coat meant, and the answer was, "My daughter, the coat is my power. You will be clothed with the Holy Spirit when you obey me. The Holy Spirit has power and transforms people." I used to complain about being a pastor's wife, but this no longer bothers me since I decided to go into the ministry myself. I finally realized after all those years that my husband was on the right path and I was not.

18) The Driver

There was a homeless man in Glasgow. I did not have any attraction for the man, but in my dream, I loved him. Because I loved him, somehow I lost my driver's license. Now I had a driver who took me to different places.

I asked the Lord about the meaning of the dream. The answer came, "My daughter, you loved the world, which is not worthy of your love, but you did anyway. Now because of your love for the world, you have lost your privilege of driving. When you drive, you go to the wrong places. I am giving you a new driver, the Holy Spirit, to lead you where you should go and to do what I want you to do."

My final decision to serve God came when I realized that I would no longer be doing His work by my power, my strength, or my wisdom, but by God's power through the Holy Spirit. This dream occurred after I started asking God to help me to clearly hear the Holy Spirit's leading. God proved to me that the Holy Spirit is true and is capable of helping me to do God's work.

19) The Evil Spirit

I met a woman who believed in a traveling spirit. While she was explaining her experience, I suddenly felt very uneasy. I silently inquired of God whether her spiritual experience was coming from God. After praying, I felt a strange feeling all over my body and wanted to leave that place fast. I thought something was wrong but did not know what.

When I told this story to my mother, she told me that she felt a chill all over. My mother understood what I was saying. She understands my spiritual experiences more than anyone else I know.

She can tell other people's spiritual condition when she prays, even if she does not know the person. That evening I had a dream in which I saw two trees on the sidewalk and one tree planted on the paved road. I thought if a car ran into the tree planted on the road, both the car and the tree would get damaged.

I asked the Lord about this dream and the answer came, "My daughter, the tree on the road is the woman whom you have asked about. Her source of power comes from the devil." A couple of days later, I had another dream about her. She was standing before me, and suddenly a big, tall devil appeared behind her and tried to attack me. I told the devil to leave in Jesus' name. I knew I was winning because I was relying on Jesus.

After I awoke, I realized the power of Jesus. I cannot win the battle by myself but I win when I rely on Jesus. The woman was searching and thought her spiritual condition was right. It is easy to be deceived by the devil if a person is searching for God only from spiritual experience but does not have much knowledge of the Scriptures. She said she had access to wonderful spiritual experiences without studying the Scriptures. I learned the importance of knowing God's Word.

20) A Fire

One day when I visited The Iliff School of Theology, I was in tears because I felt I should be in school to prepare to go into the ministry but I was not able to because of my husband's opposition. During one of the services, I felt Jesus was sitting in front of me listening to all my hurts and thoughts. Then Jesus told me that I needed to pray for my husband because he was going through a very difficult time. I decided to pray for 100 days for one hour every morning.

Then I had a dream about fire. Our house was connected to the church. I kept piling crumpled papers next to the oven. When my husband and I saw a little fire starting, we both tried to put it out. Then another fire started where my papers were. When I saw a gas pipe right next to the stove, I panicked. I understood that the fire I saw was the Holy Spirit's purifying work in people's hearts, and my decision to pray for my husband had something to do with cleansing.

21) The Worshippers

I had a dream that my husband and I were walking around in a hallway at The Iliff School of Theology. The floor was dirty, and everywhere we turned, I saw garbage. The bathroom had toilet paper all over the floor. My husband told me that he was right about the school being a mess and was trying to discourage me from going there. As we walked along, I opened doors and saw people worshipping God in reverence. Their faces were all touching the floor and praying.

After I woke up, I was convinced that some of the teaching at Iliff might originate from human knowledge and not from Christian principles. However, many people who come to school there believe in God and have a heart for Him. That dream gave me confidence that God would be with me, teaching me, even though (some people think) Iliff is perhaps a little too liberal.

22) A New Church

On the 91st day after I committed to praying for my husband, I dreamt that my husband and I were in a new church. He was greeting a new congregation and I was looking up at him with love and respect.

I asked God what the dream meant because my husband was not planning to move with me to Denver but was going to stay in Glasgow. God spoke to my heart, "My daughter, I am going to move your husband." Three days after I had this dream, I was sitting in Bible study. As I was looking at my husband who was sitting across from me, God showed me an image. I saw a middle-sized tree and a hand with a scoop trying to dig it out. I asked God for the meaning, and the answer came, "My daughter, I am going to move your husband." On the 99th day after I started praying for my husband, he got a phone call from the district superintendent asking him if he wanted to move to Wyoming which would be about half the distance to my school. My husband agreed to move. I was upset that God had not changed my husband's mind about moving to Denver. When I complained about this, God spoke to my heart, "I have answered your prayers. You asked me to help your family move to a place where you all can grow spiritually." God was right. I grew because I had to drive so many hours in which I was able to spend more quality time with Him. Because of our hardships, tears, pain and suffering, our family grew.

23) Dirty Dishes

The very first night after my husband and I were introduced to the church in Wyoming, I had a dream. I was walking through the church we had visited that evening. There were a lot of dirty dishes, but no one was there to wash them. I felt it was not my responsibility to wash them. When I turned the corner, I saw a big black dog that scared me. Because of that dream, I felt sure that God was leading us to move to that church because there was a lot of work to be done. Praying would be part of the work. The dog I saw in my dream symbolized problems which would come up at that church in the future.

4. Dreams after I started attending The Iliff School of Theology

24) My Shoes

In many of my dreams, I was searching for shoes because I had somehow lost them. Once, I went searching for shoes among the pastors, and I could not find them. I awoke and asked God what that meant. The shoes represented the ministries that God has called me to. I had not yet found the ministry work that God had prepared for me to do. After I started attending The Iliff School of Theology, I had another dream about shoes. I was going on a long bicycle journey and was wearing sandals. I knew I had to wear better shoes, so I looked around and found one of my white shoes but could not find the other one. When I finally found a second shoe, it did not match the first one.

God said, "My daughter, when you are looking for shoes you are searching for my dreams, visions and hopes for you. My dreams, visions and hopes of what kind of person and worker you should be are your shoes, which will lead you to do what I want you to do." Since then, I pray that I will understand God's dreams, visions and hopes for me, and that I will do what God asks.

25) A Mentor

I dreamt that my daughter was dating another man. After I

woke up, I could not understand why I had this dream. My daughter was dating a man at the time, so this dream was from God to warn me about what was going to happen to her.

That morning, I went to church to pray. God told me that my daughter needed a mentor because difficult times were coming. I never thought about finding a mentor for my daughter until that day. God told me that I needed to ask Michelle Hannan to be her mentor. I drove to Denver to attend school, and that night I called Michelle and asked her if she could mentor my daughter. She told me that when our church was talking about mentoring, she immediately thought about my daughter and she would be glad to do it.

For many years, all through my daughter's high school years, Michelle took my daughter to her home, fixed a meal for her and spent time with her every Wednesday night. I will be forever thankful for what Michelle has done. Not long after Michelle started mentoring her, my daughter and her boyfriend broke up, and she went through a very difficult time. I was not able to help my daughter because I was gone a lot, but Michelle was able to. I thanked God for helping my daughter. She had a tough time during her teenage years, and God helped her through Michelle. She was always willing to take my daughter in her arms and carry her through. I will always be grateful for her generous and nurturing spirit.

For the three years I attended seminary, I was home on the weekends, except for summer and winter vacation. Attending winter quarter was a challenge for me. I wanted to be home for the weekends with my family. Due to winter storms, sometimes I would have to turn around and in tears drive back to Denver. Before I started school, God asked me for a 100 percent commitment to serve Him, and I said I would do it. I realized later why He asked me for my total commitment. If I had not done that, people around me might have changed my mind. Many people did not understand my calling and thought I should stay home to take care of my kids. I knew my family needed me. No one understood how I felt during those days. I could not even explain it because I felt so much opposition.

Why did I respond to His calling during my family's critical times? God had given me the urgency to respond to spreading the gospel, and He assured me that He would take care of my family. I thought my husband would be able to take care of our two children.

However, he had a very difficult time. Giving my fears and worries for my family to God was not easy. I knew my life, my marriage, and my family were in God's hands. I had to do what He was telling me. I had to trust God for everything. I shed many tears in those days, but God encouraged me to stay on course, and I am glad He took care of my children.

26) The Trees

I had a dream that I was walking through a place where colorful trees were displaying their beauty. It was so awesome and marvelous that I could feel the beauty in my spirit. I've never experienced beauty in that way. This was something new to me. When I got close to the trees, I was surprised to find out that they were artificial.

I asked the Lord about this and the answer came, "My daughter, the beauty you see in people, their knowledge, and any other beauty that you see in this world is more like those artificial trees when compared to God's beauty." After I started attending Iliff, I met many wonderful professors and students. I admired their knowledge and academic abilities. This dream reminded me that my focus always should be on God and not on people's wisdom.

27) A Strong Man

The first time I went to a prison to give testimony, I felt more blessed than ever. The Holy Spirit touched people's hearts, including mine. Two days later, I had the worst dream I have ever had. I was getting beat up by two strong men. I had such a difficult time. I said, "Blood of Jesus, protect me," but I felt I was losing.

After I woke up, I told my husband about the terrible dream. I told him that some spiritual beings were attacking me in my dream. I was sure that those two men were not ordinary men. I felt weak as though someone had really beaten me. I went back to sleep, and the next dream was worse than the first. A huge man, much taller and bigger than the two men I had seen in my previous dream, was trying to kill me. I knew that if that man caught me I would get hurt. I ran into a room where a mother and a daughter were. When I thought I could go out, this huge strong man was waiting outside to try to kill me again. I shut the first door and locked it, but the man broke it open. The next door where the mother and the little girl were did not have a lock. I asked the mother to hold the door. The man was trying to push the door open, but the mother obviously was strong. The man pushed open the top part, and I could see his face. I was trying to hit him with something, but I was not strong enough. The man was much stronger than we were. I was glad that I woke up.

God was showing me that the little girl in my dream was me, and my mother's prayer was protecting me. I was still a little child spiritually and I needed to grow and be strong. I asked the Lord about this dream. "My daughter, Satan's attack on my children is real, especially for those who are doing my work. Warn others about this." After I had this dream, I knew that prison ministry is what I needed to do. I felt that I would not be able to do prison work unless I spent time praying and fasting. I have to be strong spiritually in order to encourage those who are in prison to rely on Jesus and not themselves. I believe the devil was trying to discourage me from going into prison ministry, but I know that is where God's grace is outpouring. I understood then why God was asking me to fast from time to time. I need to be strong spiritually to minister to people in prison because the devil does not want to lose anyone to Jesus.

28) The Harvest

In my dream, a Korean man with a turnip came and told me the price. The price was so high that I thought if I could plant lots of turnips, I would be able to make lots of money. Suddenly, I saw myself standing in a large golden field with grain ready for harvest. The heads of grain were heavy and making waves in the blowing wind. Instantly, I thought if I could plant the turnips in that huge field, I could make lots of money. But there was no time to dig or plant the turnips. The field was ready for harvest.

I had this dream about a week after I went to a prison to give my testimony. I asked God about the meaning, and His reply was, "My daughter, I am sending you to the prisons where the fields are ready for harvest. You did not plant. You did not tend the field, but I am sending you so you can harvest as my worker. Go, I will go with you and show you wonders. I will open people's hearts and save them. The price you must pay is to willingly go where I send you. Volunteer to give your testimony in different prisons." I gave my testimony in eight different jails and prisons while attending Iliff. I have been more blessed because of prison ministry. God's Spirit is helping many people in prisons.

29) A Professor

I had a dream about a professor from The Iliff School of Theology. I saw her from afar, but was able to see her face as though I were very close to her. Her car was about to fall into a river. The car's back wheels were at the edge of a bridge, and she was trying to pull the car onto the bridge by herself. I knew that even if I tried to help her, there was no way the car would move, so I did not help her. While the professor was trying to move the car, she somehow scooped the dirty water with her hands and drank it.

I asked God about the meaning of the dream and the reply came, "My daughter, the professor thinks that she has a car. The car is her way of thinking about salvation. But she cannot move because she does not have the right car. She cannot help others because she does not have any way of showing others the way. The dirty water is worldly knowledge which does not come from me." This woman professor was teaching the Bible but she was not a Christian.

30) A Spirit of Despair

Just before I went out to a men's prison to give a testimony, I had a dream about a man I knew. He was suicidal and talked about how he was disappointed with God. He was blaming God for not helping him and was filled with despair. I tried to comfort him.

I asked the Lord about this dream and the reply came, "My daughter, there are many people suffering in prison with the spirit of despair and suicide. Tell them that I love them and will help them if they rely on me. They can only win this spiritual battle when they rely on my name to cast out the evil spirits. What I give them is peace, not torment." This dream gave me one more reason to go to prisons and give my testimony to encourage people.

31) Searching

In a dream I was visiting a friend of mine, Sue, a nurse in the hospital where I was trying to find work. The steps in that hospital were made of metal and were very steep. I told Sue that I should give up looking for a job at that hospital because I have problems with heights and the hospital was too small. Sue and I went anyway. A nurse gave Sue a little decorated angel that had a heart shape that tells a person's mood. When Sue pressed the button, it showed her mood. The nurse said, "Sue's heart seems to be happy and energized." By the time we were leaving the hospital, the nurse told Sue that she should throw away the little pretty gift she received. I said, "I wish I could have it if she has to throw it away." I liked angels. Then I realized that the angel decoration was on her head. I had never seen anything like that. The nurse said that she would solve the problem and brought out a larger pretty gift that was decorated with angels. I thought she was going to just give it to me, but she spread it out and it turned into a feast table, like a big buffet and she started distributing the food.

God gave me understanding of this dream as I recorded it: I had applied to St. Anthony's Hospital residency program. The director said that they were offering me a chaplain job over the phone. I thought I had the job. I thought I would be starting when I had finished my first Clinical Pastoral Education. I was disappointed when it did not work out. I was still trying to find a ministry after I finished seminary. I wish I had this dream before I got the phone call, then I would have been prepared. I only trusted my own experiences and what the director told me. In most cases, I had gotten whatever job that I interviewed for, so I expected that I would get this job not realizing God had different plans for me.

During this time, my friend, Mi Cha, told me that she had dreamt about me. In her dream, my two legs had been amputated and my son was taking care of my wounds. While I was listening to her, God told me that I would not get this hospital residency job. Moreover, her dream told me that I was going to have a difficult time finding the right ministry.

Mi Cha's dream was right. As I was waiting to be appointed to a ministry, I had a difficult time and my son encouraged me during that time. My son even helped me when I was attending seminary. One day I was crying because we had so many rentals, and my manager told me about all these problems with them; but we did not have the money to fix them. I told my son, "I am so sorry that you are suffering financially because I bought so many rental houses." He tried to encourage me saying, "Mom, even though you have problems with money, you shouldn't feel so bad. Think about how many people you are helping through your prison ministry." I thanked him for saying that. My son is perceptive, brilliant, and compassionate. He encouraged me the most when I was having a difficult time.

After I finished school, we moved to Keenesburg and my son helped me again. Just having him around me was encouraging since I was not able to spend much time with him when I was attending seminary. I told him, "You are my joy." We had many bills piling up in those days and I felt helpless and hopeless. God spoke to my heart and encouraged me. "My daughter, I want you to proclaim victory every day. You will see that victory. You will taste that victory. You will see others' transformations. Only then will you be transformed."

So, I learned to proclaim victory in Jesus, even though our financial situation was worse after I graduated from the seminary. While attending school, I received so many scholarships that we did better financially. After I finished school, I thought Rocky Mountain Conference of the United Methodist Church Bishop would appoint me to work as a minister in a church, but I didn't receive any calls. I believe this was all God's plan. He was not opening the door me to work as a parish minister, but eventually I would be working as a chaplain, but at that point, I didn't quite understand it.

This is what I wrote during that time: "Things are going badly in our home, especially with our finances. The bills are piling up. We don't even have enough money to buy food. We do have some food at home, but I feel bad that I could not buy my son what he wanted to eat. He wanted to eat hot wings from Walmart, but I did not have the money to buy them. That hurts me. I do not even open the bills these days, knowing that we don't have enough money to pay them. My husband's income tax report said we owed money and we do not have the money to pay it. But, I have learned to proclaim victory in Christ. All the problems with finances will be solved eventually. They are temporary problems because everything in this life is temporary. I need to find work, but I feel going back to my old computer profession is almost like Peter going back to fishing after Jesus was crucified. Peter caught nothing all night long. Only Jesus can tell me where to catch the fish now. I feel ministry is what I am called to do, and that's where I need to cast the net. So, I am waiting for God's leading."

When I was hurting badly, I started reciting one of my favorite Scriptures from *Acts 2:17-18: "In the last days, God says, I will pour out my Spirit on all people. Your sons and daughters will prophesy, your young men will see visions, your old men will dream dreams. Even on my servants, both men and women, I will pour out my Spirit in those days, and they will prophesy."*

During that time, my sister sent me a nice suit saying, that I needed to wear a nice suit when I preached. I was grateful for her thoughtfulness. I did not have the money to buy new clothes and God provided what I needed. That was God's grace.

When I asked God about my job, He spoke to my heart, "Someone will call you and I will take care of you." God was right. Someone called and offered me the medical interpreter's job which paid well, and soon after that I got a part-time job as the hospital Chaplain. I have been able to handle our finances since then. God spoke to me one day to encourage me while I was waiting for my ministry work. He said, "I have many people working for me and I will take care of you."

However, I was not satisfied with the interpreter's job, because I was not able to use my ministry skills. In my dream, I did not get what I wanted and I had to see what God wanted to do through my ministry. As I look back, it was a good thing that I did not get the job at St. Anthony's because it was only a one-year residency position but this other hospital chaplain position turned out better in the long run because it was not a temporary job. God knew what was best for me. God helped me with our finances and opened the doors of ministry for me more than I've ever imagined.

5. Dreams after I started working at ACDF

32) A Baby

I had a dream that I was working in a hospital and a baby girl needed a diaper change. I was told that I was responsible for providing the diapers. My director was changing her messy diaper and I was searching all over for a diaper. I looked all over, but I was not able to find one. Finally, I found a pink diaper for the baby girl.

The director changed the diaper. In the dream I understood that the baby girl represented one of the chaplains who just started working at the hospital at the time.

When I had this dream, God told me that I was going to have problems with a new chaplain who started working at the hospital where I worked. He spoke to me, "My daughter, I wanted to prepare your heart." God was right. The next day I was meeting with the hospital director for my work evaluation. Suddenly I remembered my dream and I knew there would be some trouble coming up because of this new chaplain. My work evaluation was fine, but I knew there was something that I had to resolve with my director. I asked the director if there was anything else he had to say to me. He mentioned the new chaplain whom God had mentioned in my dream. He said that this new chaplain said something hurtful about me. He told me to visit her and resolve it because things were out of control. She blamed me for something I did not do.

That was just the beginning of the trouble. The director was not sure who was telling the truth. I suggested that we needed another party to resolve this problem since the director was not able to, but that did not help. I was working three nights a week at the hospital, and I also worked as a medical interpreter part-time. I was satisfied with my income even though I felt I was not using my spiritual gifts to the fullest.

Not long after that, the director cut my hours to two nights and gave more hours to the new chaplain. Because of that, I had to work more hours as a medical interpreter. Even though the interpretation job paid well, I was not happy because I was not able to use my ministry gifts and skills. I knew my calling was prison ministry, so I called the chaplain at ACDF so I could be a volunteer. I had spent time talking with the ACDF chaplain while I was in seminary. I was told that he was not a chaplain there anymore so the jail was looking for chaplains. I was told to apply. I did and started working as a chaplain at ACDF in December 2003. I have been blessed since I started this job. I knew God led me to minister to the incarcerated, and I was able to use my spiritual gifts to the fullest. I could not be happier. God also opened my ministry opportunities more than ever through a prison ministry book project.

God was leading through all of this. If the director had not cut my hours, I would not have had to look for another job because I was satisfied with my pay. About a year later, the hospital chaplain that I had problems with had problems with the director as well. The director apologized to me saying that he had misunderstood me. He said he felt bad about what happened to me. I thanked him for letting me know how he felt. I also I thanked him for cutting my hours because God then opened the doors for me to minister to the incarcerated more than ever before.

About a year later, I had a dream about this woman again. I was in this hospital with her, and she threw all our shoes out on the street. I lost my shoes which had shoe laces. I saw a man who was wearing a shoe with shoe laces. I thought he had stolen mine, but he hadn't.

Shoes in my dreams seems to indicate my ministry. God spoke to my heart, "Let go of her. She isn't the one who let you lose your shoes, but it's I who let you lose them, so I could give you something else." I thanked God that I had problems with this woman so I was able to move on to find the prison ministry. Moreover, I learned how to bless and forgive others because of the lesson I learned through this experience. God taught me to bless others instead of having resentments when they hurt me. The devil had no control of my mind because I would bless her whenever I thought about her. I thank God for that lesson. God taught me that good things can come out of bad things, and this was one of those cases.

33) The Voices from Hell

Not long after I started working at ACDF as a chaplain, I had a dream that I heard voices of torment from hell. I asked the Lord why I had this dream where I had heard the painful screams. God told me, "My daughter, time is short. Many do not have much time, but they do not realize it. Preach the gospel. They need to be saved from eternal burning hell. Many will be grieving when the time comes, you need to warn them." Many people do not believe in eternal hell which is prepared for those who do not believe in Jesus. Many believe their own reasons why there is no hell but they do not take into account what Jesus said about hell in the Bible.

This dream gave me more motivation to share the gospel of Jesus. If I can save only one more person from going to hell by sharing the gospel, I have to do it. I pray everyone who reads this believes in Jesus and can be saved. Peter said, *"Salvation is found in no one else, for there is no other name under heaven given to men by which we must be saved." (Acts 4:12)* If you have not accepted Jesus as your Savior and Lord, do not delay any more. You might not have much time left. Pray to him to forgive your sins and ask Jesus to come into your heart.

34) A Call

I had a dream that God was revealing to me that one of the Bible study leaders at ACDF was called to the ministry. God told me, "Tell him he is called to the ministry. Mentor him while he is at ACDF and let him preach. Tell him unless he walks the right path and follows his calling, he will be coming back to jail. He might have to go to prison, but that will only purify him more." I told this man that he was called to the ministry and gave him the chance to preach in chaplain's worship services. He was an excellent preacher and helped many. He was sentenced to community corrections, backslid, and came back to our facility. He struggled a lot and looked so lost. Again, God spoke to me to encourage him to preach. I spoke to him about how he can come out of despair by serving God. He started preaching and started helping others. He started coming out of depression because he was focusing on God. He went to DOC, but I was glad that he finally started focusing on serving God instead of focusing on what he had lost in his life.

35) The Train

In this dream I was desperate to catch a train to "Chun An" in Korea. Interestingly, Chun means "Heaven." I paid $50 for the ticket, but I got there late and missed the train. I was so disappointed.

God spoke to me about this dream. "My daughter, that's how many people will feel later if they do not follow me." I learned that many times we ignore the Holy Spirit's leading, and I felt this feeling of regret when I ignored the Holy Spirit speaking to my heart one day. It happened when I was giving a presentation at the Women's Minimum Correctional Center in Pueblo. I was the main speaker and my friend was in charge of leading prayer. I ignored God when He told me to pray for people who were suffering with addiction. I ignored the Holy Spirit's voice twice, thinking, I was not the one who was leading prayer. While we were driving back home, God told me that I should have obeyed Him and prayed for people who suffer with addiction. Then I realized that I should have listened to Him instead of coming up with an excuse why I should not do it. I asked God to forgive me.

36) A Donut Shop

I had a donut shop in a dream and I was sitting on top of a big donut which looked like a black tire. When I sat on top of it, it would fly and I was enjoying it. It was fun and I had not seen anything like it.

God spoke to my heart, "My daughter, it is the Holy Spirit who will be able to take you to a place which is unbelievable and unimaginable for you. I will let you know that it is the Holy Spirit's power that will lift you and lead you to different places." I knew God was reminding me that the Holy Spirit is the One who helped me in my ministry.

37) A Woman

In a dream, a woman came and told me that she saw a demon and was scared of it.

God warned me, "My daughter, the spiritual world is real but many do not know about it. They are beaten down by the devil and do not even realize that it is happening. Warn them and teach them. I have overcome the devil, and my children need to learn to fight the spiritual battle by living a holy life."

When we accept the devil's sinful suggestions, we fall into sin. We need to learn to resist all the temptations which will lead us into sin. We have to choose to live a holy and acceptable life in order to have a clear conscience before God, so the devil won't have anything to accuse us of having done. The devil puts us in bondage to guilt and shame. The devil will try to plant destructive thoughts in our minds and will tell us to follow the destructive path. We need to resist any thoughts that will make us turn our back on God and hurt ourselves or others, so we can win the spiritual battle. The devil will try to make us fall into sin, and that's when we feel we are trapped.

38) Mentoring Leaders

I had a dream that a man came to me and showed me a baby girl and asked me to mentor her. It seemed I had met this man and the baby girl somewhere before, but I could not remember where. I had a difficult time saying yes to his request because I was so busy with my ministry.

God told me how to handle it. "My daughter, you could mentor many more people. I will send you people who can help you mentor others. You need to mentor leaders so they can mentor others." God spoke to my heart to train leaders from the beginning of my ministry. Because of that, I try to find leaders and mentor them. One way I have been doing that is to encourage inmate leaders to prepare testimonies and sermons to preach in chaplain's worship services. While they are preparing to preach, the Holy Spirit will lead them in what to share. Maximum Saints books are the result of the inmate leaders' ministry in our facility. If I can help them to use their gifts to the fullest, they can help many others. If I am overwhelmed, that means I am not mentoring leaders, but mentoring too many baby Christians. I cannot be effective if I have to take care of too many babies. I thank God for this lesson.

39) The Dried Dirt

I had a dream that God showed me dried dirt in a pot.

I asked God about it and He said, "People without the Holy Spirit are like dried dirt in a pot. The soil is not ready to plant. There is no fruit and there is no way a seed can grow."

I realized how important it is to experience the Holy Spirit and learn how to hear the voice of God in our spiritual journey. Without the Holy Spirit starting to break the hard soil in our hearts, through the conviction of our sins, the seed of God's Word cannot grow in us. People who do not learn how to listen to God's voice do not have clear direction of how to serve God. I believe that through prayer, we can have a deeper relationship with Jesus and the Holy Spirit.

Many do not understand why people weep in worship or while praying, but tears are a blessing from God. When the Holy Spirit is present, people start weeping. The Holy Spirit has started healing some areas that we may not even understand. We begin to understand something that we could not understand before. When that happens, we are overwhelmed and we cannot help but weep. Weeping in the presence of God is like watering for the garden and breaking the hard soil for planting. I wept for a year whenever I went to pray before I finally made a decision to go into the ministry. I was weeping so much that I was concerned about my eyes. I was crying because I did not want to go in the ministry, but the Holy Spirit was changing my heart. At the time, some people told me that tears are a blessing from God and I did not understand what they were saying. Later, after God healed my heart, changing it from a stubborn one to an obedient one, I understood what they were saying. God was breaking my hardened heart so that He could plant the seeds of faith and obedience there. I see hope when people weep before the Lord. Breaking our hearts is a painful process that is necessary for transformation. Changing our perception and our lifestyle is hard but it's absolutely necessary in our spiritual growth.

Part Five:
Prayer Project

Drawing "Armor of God" by Bobbie Michel

1. A 30-Day Prayer Project:
Healing from Nightmares

Who can participate in this prayer project?

This prayer project is for those who are suffering from nightmares and for those who want to find peace. Many people have no peace whether they are awake or asleep, and some are afraid to go to sleep because of nightmares. They feel helpless and wonder why they suffer so much.

Jesus said, *"Peace I leave with you, my peace I give you. I do not give to you as the world gives. Do not let your hearts be troubled and do not be afraid." (John 14:27)* Jesus is the Prince of Peace, and wants us to have peace all the time. The peace Jesus provides for us is a blessing in this troubled world. Many people, even those who proclaim that they are Christians, do not have peace.

This prayer project is to help you learn to have peace whether you are awake or asleep. Remember, there is no shortcut for this spiritual path of finding peace. Spiritual discipline takes time, and it is hard work. There are many areas you need to work on to keep this peace. Sometimes, you need to change your way of thinking, speaking, and behaving in order to have peace. Ask the Holy Spirit to guide you and help you understand the Bible and understand yourself. In this way, you can be freed from worries, torment, and fear. For the next 30 days, every day, read the Bible for 30 minutes and pray for 30 minutes; talk to God for 15 minutes and listen to God for 15 minutes, then follow the reflection, meditation, and prayers suggested here. If you cannot find peace and be freed from nightmares in the first 30 days, I suggest that you do another 30 days, then as many more days as you need to until you have found peace.

Finding peace and keeping that peace are two different things. Jesus offers peace to all by inviting us to walk with him. But staying on that path is a lifelong process of learning through obedience. Many times we take the path of destruction and lose peace. The good news is that even if we lose peace, we can go back and find it because God's grace is greater than our weaknesses. We lose peace because there may be areas we need to change. We need God's wisdom and strength to make changes. Jesus said, *"Everything is possible for Him who believes." (Mark 9:23)* Prayer: "God, help me to find peace in you, not only when I am awake, but in my sleep as well. Help others who are suffering from nightmares, so they will be delivered from the spirit of torment and fear and be filled with the Spirit of peace. In the name of Jesus I pray. Amen."

1. Spiritual exercises which will help you when you suffer from nightmares.

Sometimes we do not quite understand why we are having bad dreams. I know they make people feel helpless and hopeless. I am thankful that my mother was there to instruct me about my bad dreams. When you are having nightmares, there may be many reasons. Through dreams, we can see the spiritual condition of our souls. If we are not standing strong in our faith, the devil will try to torment us with destructive thoughts, attitudes and dreams.

Not all dreams are the work of the Holy Spirit. Even though God wants us to repent when we fall into sin, I don't believe God punishes people through their dreams. God does not terrorize anyone by giving them bad dreams, but we do encounter the spiritual realm. We need to put on the full armor of God to win the spiritual battle. Also, not all bad dreams are the work of the devil. The Holy Spirit may be warning us about what is going to happen in the future and that we need to pray.

Spiritual war is real. Those who have received the gift of spiritual discernment can see and feel the devil's attack. The devil can torment people. Therefore, not all spiritual encounters are the work of the Holy Spirit.

We can win the battle, however, if we follow the instruction of the Scriptures. Peter wrote, *"Humble yourselves, therefore, under God's mighty hand, that he may lift you up in due time. Cast all your anxiety on him because he cares for you. Be self-controlled and alert. Your enemy the devil prowls around like a roaring lion looking for someone to devour. Resist him, standing firm, in the faith, because you know that your brothers throughout the world are undergoing the same kind of sufferings." (1 Peter 5:6-9)*

To win this battle I encourage you to follow these spiritual exercises. I ask you to accept Jesus as your Lord and Savior if you have not already done so. Do not expect Jesus to help you if you do not have a relationship with Him. Here is a prayer so you can invite

Jesus into your heart and be strong enough in the Lord to win even the spiritual battles in your dreams:

(1) Learn about God's ways: Start reading the Bible, either the Gospel of John or Romans. While reading, see if there is anything you need to ask God to forgive. Ask Him to forgive you and ask Jesus to wash you with His blood to cleanse you of your sin. Ask God to give you the strength to live a holy life. We lose peace because of our sins, so try not to repeat your mistakes. Ask the Holy Spirit to give you the wisdom to understand the Bible and learn about God's ways.

(2) Ask the Holy Spirit to help you cleanse your life: The Holy Spirit is a gift to all Christians. When you accept Jesus, the Holy Spirit will be with you to teach, direct, guide, counsel, and comfort you. Ask Jesus to help you live a godly life.

(3) Forgive everyone who has sinned against you, including yourself: Many of us are hurting because we have been wronged by others. We need to forgive them and learn to let go of anger and resentment. Start blessing people who hurt you and start asking God to help you forgive. God will give you peace when you forgive.

(4) Pray to God to help you experience healing: If you have been abused or are a victim of violence, you need to experience healing from God. Ask Him to help you let go of your resentments and anger. Pray, so God can give you wisdom to let go of the painful memories. The devil will tell you that you do not have to forgive, but do not listen to him. Rely on Jesus to fight the devil's lies. If you do not forgive, you will open the door for the devil to hurt you more. If you see a demon in your dream, rebuke the devil to leave in Jesus' name. Keep reading the Bible and pray so you will be strong.

(5) Do not justify your sinful attitudes and behaviors: The devil tries to tell our minds that it is all right to sin, but do not listen to his suggestions. Whatever suggestions come from the Holy Spirit to our minds are to help us grow. The devil's suggestions always sound good, but they invite us to fall into sin. This is not going to help us get closer to God, rather it will hinder our growth and in the process, we will lose peace only to end up in turmoil.

(6) <u>Go to church and get to know other Christians who can help you</u>: If you feel weak like a newborn baby in Christ, you need to find others who can help you understand the Bible. They know what you are going through and have learned how to fight the spiritual battle. Do not be discouraged if you cannot find a mentor right away. The Holy Spirit is a divine person who lives in you and will help you.

(7) <u>Learn to clear your mind and to resist all the bad thoughts that come to you</u>: You can learn to control your destructive thoughts and start praying more, so the devil will not have room to attack you. *(2 Corinthians 10:5)* You need to resist destructive thoughts and rebuke them in the name of Jesus. Quickly turn your mind to the powerful Word of God, He will help you in this process. It might take some time to win the battle of controlling your thoughts. In Jesus' name and in faith, you need to fill your mind with the powerful Word of God. The Holy Spirit within you is strong and will teach you, but you must learn to obey the Lord.

(8) <u>Dedicate your time to prayer and Scripture reading for an hour every day for 30 days</u>: I encourage you to do a 30-day prayer with a strong commitment to know Jesus. Read the gospel and pray that you will be set free from all nightmares. Bad dreams may not disappear right away, but as time passes you will be stronger and the devil will know that. Keep focusing your heart on Jesus if things do not improve. Try to follow Jesus so the devil has to flee, not only when you are awake, but also in your dreams. We need to learn to focus our hearts and minds on Christ to win the spiritual battle. Do not let the devil scare you because you are stronger than he is when you rely on Jesus.

(9) <u>Try to serve God by serving others</u>: We will only grow if we obey the Lord. Jesus told us to make disciples of Christ and help others grow in faith. Taking care of the poor, underprivileged, undervalued in society and people who are hurting is our task. As we grow in faith and become a true servant of God, we will be strong spiritually and there is less of a chance that we will suffer from nightmares.

2. <u>Let's reflect on areas where we lose peace, learn how we can find it and be freed from nightmares.</u>

(1) <u>Lack of spiritual knowledge about the Bible</u>: Even if you are a Christian, you may not know the Scriptures well enough to build up your relationship with the Lord or understand the spiritual battles in your life. Start reading the Bible to get to know Jesus and ask the Holy Spirit to teach you about Jesus. God will guide you. Pray to be filled with the Holy Spirit's peace. *(Galatians 5:22-26)*

(2) <u>Lack of faith</u>: You may know the Scriptures, but may have a difficult time because you don't have faith in God. Ask God to give you a gift of faith that can move mountains. *(Matthew 17:20)*

(3) <u>Critical events in your life</u>: You may have encountered traumatic events, like losing your loved ones, that you are still grieving about and do not know how to get over. When you are emotionally upset, you are vulnerable. The devil takes advantage of these situations and torments people through their dreams. Ask God to bring healing in your heart so you can see the big picture and find peace. *(Isaiah 43:1-5)*

(4) <u>Unforgiving spirit</u>: If you are filled with anger and bitterness and do not forgive, you invite the devil to put you into a state of hate and anger. Therefore, you cannot have peace. Sometimes other people's sinful actions have traumatized you and you may have nightmares. God understands the pain and suffering you have gone through. Let go of any expectations of others you might have, bless them and pray for them. Also, forgive yourself.

(5) <u>Spiritual attack</u>: Sometimes the spirit of torment comes after you with feelings of guilt, even after you repent of your sins. The devil will tell you that God will not forgive you or love you because you are no good. He will tell you that God will not answer your prayers. Rebuke the spirit of lies to leave you in Jesus' name. *(John 10:10, 1 Peter 5:8-9, John 8:36, James 4:6-7)*

(6) <u>Sin in life</u>: God may be helping you to see your spiritual condition through dreams, so you can turn to Him and repent. Every time we fall into sin, we invite the devil to have more space in our mind and we lose our peace. We need to repent every sin we have committed and ask God for wisdom to resist

temptation. *(Luke 11:24-26)*

(7) <u>You do not have peace if you do not have Jesus in your heart</u>: If you do not have faith in Jesus, he cannot help you and you do not have the power to win the spiritual battle. You need to accept Jesus as your personal Savior and rely on His power to help you. Here is a prayer to accept Jesus. "Lord come into my heart and forgive all my sins. Fill me with the Holy Spirit and bless me with your peace. Help me to have a new heart to obey you. In Jesus' name. Amen." Remember, you have to keep following Jesus to keep peace. *(Matthew 11:28-30)*

(8) <u>Disobedient heart</u>: Many do not have peace because they do not obey God's call in their lives. Selfishness and disobedience are sin. Ignoring the Holy Spirit's direction in our life is sin. When we do not use our gifts for the glory of God, we sin. Misusing our gifts (even our lives are gifts from God) is sin. Hiding our gifts and not using them to build up the kingdom of God is sin. The Holy Spirit comes after us to convict us when we try to run away from our call to serve the Lord. If we have sin in our lives, continuing to live in that sin may cause us to lose our peace. Jonah ran away from the Lord and was disobedient. Jonah and other people suffered greatly because he ignored God's plans. You need to surrender your life completely to serve the Lord. *(Jonah 1:1-17, 2:1-2)*

(9) <u>God may be speaking to you through dreams to prepare your heart</u>: Sometimes we might have nightmares because the Holy Spirit is warning us what is going to happen in the future so we can pray for protection of ourselves and others. Also, God may be trying to prepare for the hard times ahead of us.

(10) <u>You may not have learned to listen to God's voice</u>: Many people who do not have peace do not know how to listen to God's voice and so they get frustrated. They are confused when they have problems because they have not heard from the Lord that everything will turn out all right. When God starts speaking to us He will help us understand the big picture which will give us comfort and encouragement. Ask Jesus to speak to you, then listen and obey Him. *(John 10:27-29)*

(11) <u>You may love people, material things, and sinful desires more than God</u>: When we do, we lose peace. Our physical life is

temporary and all we have is a temporary gift from God. We are called to serve God not our temporary belongings. God has to be our first love. *(Matthew 6:19-24, 10:37-39)*

(12) <u>You may not have experienced the Holy Spirit's power</u>: People who have not experienced the Holy Spirit are like people who have heard about God but never experienced being in the presence of God or felt Him in their hearts. The Holy Spirit has the power to release you from torment and fill your heart with peace. Ask the Holy Spirit to bless you with peace and other spiritual fruits.

3. Try to reflect on your spiritual condition.

When you are filled with fear, you are in a spiritual battle. You are losing ground for peace. When you have nightmares and lose peace that shows that you need to work on trusting the Lord in any circumstances. Try to answer the following questions to find out which area you need to work on to experience healing.

Understand yourself: (1) When did I start having nightmares? (2) Is there any sin in my life that I need to repent? (3) What was the event that contributed to this emotional turmoil? (4) Do I love myself and forgive myself when I fail?

Understand your relationship with others: (1) Is there anyone that you have not forgiven? (2) Have you been disappointed because of others? (3) Did you hurt others and disappoint them? (4) Do you have anyone who is a mentor to you?

Understand your relationship with God: (1) How is your relationship with the Lord? (2) Do you believe God forgives you and loves you no matter what? (3) Do you believe God is on your side? (4) What do you think God is telling you now?

4. Ten spiritual exercises that will help you find peace.

(1) <u>Your relationship with Jesus is the key to finding peace</u>: Read the Gospels (Matthew, Mark, Luke, and John) for 30 minutes every day for the next 30 days to get to know Jesus. Also, read Daniel, Romans, Psalm 23, Psalm 103, 1 Peter, 2 Peter and other Scriptures for meditation. Ask the Holy Spirit to give you wisdom to understand the Scriptures. Think about what Jesus has done for you and tell him you love him whenever you think about

him. You can use your meal time so you can remember to talk to him. While eating you can pray: "Come Lord Jesus, I love you and thank you. I praise and adore you. Let me taste your beauty, love, power, wisdom, and peace today!" *(Philippians 4:4-9, John 14:15-24, Matthew 6:25-34, Hebrews 13:6)*

(2) Develop a close relationship with the Holy Spirit through prayer: Pray 30 minutes every day for the next 30 days. Talk to God for 15 minutes, and ask the Holy Spirit to speak to you for 15 minutes. Many do not have peace because they do not know how to listen to God's voice. We talk too much and do not give the Holy Spirit time to speak to us. Prayer: "Come Holy Spirit, come and speak to me. Fill my heart with peace day and night. Deliver me from bad dreams, and surround me with angels who protect me." To those who have not experienced the Holy Spirit, clear your mind and wait for one hour every day. Ask the Holy Spirit to speak to you until you experience Him. Prayer: "Holy Spirit, come and speak to me, I am listening." Forgive yourself: If you have any sins you have not repented, ask God to forgive you and He will. He can use your weaknesses and failures to train you to be a better disciple of Jesus. If you want, you can write a letter to Jesus and ask him to forgive you. Prayer: "Lord Jesus, thank you for dying on the cross to forgive my sins. Cover me with the blood of Jesus and cleanse me of all my sins. Help me to live a holy life and help me to serve you." *(1 John 1:5-10, James 4:4-10)*

(4) Forgive others: If you are obsessed with someone or some event in the past that is disturbing you, you need to forgive so God can heal you. If you do not forgive, you are opening the gate for bitterness, resentment, and anger. Bless others who have hurt you and pray for them so you can be released from the spirit of resentment. Write a forgiveness letter, but do not mail it unless it will help others. Prayer: "Lord Jesus, I made a decision to forgive everyone who has hurt me. I bless them and pray for them. Heal my painful memories. I give my anger, bitterness, and resentment to you. Fill me with a spirit of peace and love." You may have to say this prayer many times until your bitterness turns to compassion. Jesus said, *"For in the same way you judge others, you will be judged, and with the measure you use, it will be*

measured to you. 'Why do you look at the speck of sawdust in your brother's eye and pay no attention to the plank in your own eye? How can you say to your brother, "Let me take the speck out of your eye," when all the time there is a plank in your own eye? You hypocrite, first take the plank out of your own eye, and then you will see clearly to remove the speck from your brother's eye.'" (Matthew 7:2-5)

(5) <u>Obey the Holy Spirit, but resist the devil</u>: Our mind is a spiritual battlefield. The devil plants destructive thoughts so we can fall into sin, and the Holy Spirit plants good thoughts for us to grow in faith, even if it is something small. If it is a good thing and will help you and others grow in faith, it is coming from the Holy Spirit. Obey the Spirit and know that until you obey Him, you cannot have peace. *(John 14:26-27, James 1:16-18) "When Jesus had called the Twelve together, he gave them power and authority to drive out all demons and to cure diseases, and he sent them out to preach the kingdom of God and to heal the sick." (Luke 9:1-2)* Jesus gave us the power and authority to drive out demons. Watch what you think in your mind every moment. Recognize your weaknesses; then you will know which demon is after you. Rebuke any destructive thoughts and suggestions that can hurt you and others. It is not coming from the Lord. "In the name of Jesus, all the spirits that are not of God, spirit of lies, anger, resentment, bitterness, deception, fear, worry, destruction and violence, leave from me. I made a decision to forgive and bless everyone."

(6) <u>Write down your dreams and ask God for interpretations</u>: The devil can torment people through their dreams. But as we grow in faith and walk closely with Jesus, we can win the spiritual battle and be freed from nightmares. One of the signs of being filled with the Holy Spirit is having dreams, because God speaks to people through dreams. They can teach us about our spiritual condition so we will know what to do to grow in faith; they can tell us about what is going to happen in the future. Write down your dreams and ask God to give you understanding. You might not get an answer right away, if you are not familiar with how God speaks to you. If you wait long enough, He will speak to you. God can speak to us with or without words. Prayer: "As you

have revealed dreams to Daniel, please give me wisdom, knowledge, under-standing, and revelation to understand what you are telling me through dreams." *(Daniel 2:1-49, James 1:5)*

(7) <u>Speak the words that create peace, faith, victory</u>: Think before you speak. Peter wrote, *"Whoever would love life and see good days must keep his tongue from evil and his lips from deceitful speech. He must turn from evil and do good; he must seek peace and pursue it. For the eyes of the Lord are on the righteous and his ears are attentive to their prayer, but the face of the Lord is against those who do evil." (1 Peter 3:10-12)* Don't say defeating words or anything negative about yourself or others. Speak as though Jesus is standing right in front of you. Write a prayer of victory for yourself, your family, and your ministry. Prayer: "God teach me to say the words that will glorify you and help others to grow in faith. Anoint me with words of wisdom so that when I speak, I will build up God's kingdom and encourage others to grow in faith. Let me be a blessing to everyone who hears me." *(James 1:19-27)*

(8) <u>Put God first in your life</u>: Jesus said, *"Seek God and His kingdom first," (Matthew 6:33)* We need to watch for whatever consumes our mind and heart. We cannot love people or things more than God. We are called to make disciples of Jesus and teach others to obey the Lord. *"Then Jesus came to them and said, 'All authority in heaven and on earth has been given to me. Therefore go and make disciples of all nations, baptizing them in the name of the Father and of the Son and of the Holy Spirit, and teaching them to obey everything I have commanded you. And surely I am with you always, to the very end of the age.'" (Matthew 28:18-20)* Prayer: "Lord, enlarge my vision and mission to serve you with my gifts to the maximum to bring many people to Christ so they can be saved and find peace with you."

(9) <u>Meditation</u>: *"Do not let your hearts be troubled. Trust in God; trust also in me. In my Father's house are many rooms; if it were not so, I would have told you. I am going there to prepare a place for you. And if I go and prepare a place for you, I will come back and take you to be with me that you also may be where I am .... I am the way and the truth and the life. No one comes to the Father except through me." (John 14:1-3,6)*

(10)<u>Proclaim victory in every situation</u>: What we proclaim in Christ will make a difference in our spiritual journey and it will affect our thinking and behavior. It will also affect our life not only when we are awake but when we are asleep. Claiming victory in Christ shows that we do believe in God to help us handle all our difficult situations. Even if you don't see it, it is important to exercise our faith through words.

2. A 30-Day Prayer Project:

How to Listen to God's Voice and Find Direction in Life

One of the most frequent questions I have been asked in my ministry is, "How can I learn to listen to God's voice?" That's the reason I created this prayer project. Jesus told his disciples to wait for the Holy Spirit, and it took 50 days of waiting to experience the Holy Spirit. When the Holy Spirit came, the disciples' lives were transformed. Their ministry was not led by their timid, fearful hearts, but with boldness and the guidance of the Holy Spirit.

I learned that listening in prayer is more important than talking to God. Think about what will happen when God speaks to you? You will be transformed. If you don't recognize God's leading and His clear voice, you are missing a lot. I cannot stress enough on listening because listening prayer has changed my life. Relationship is the key in our spiritual growth. When God starts revealing things to you, your understanding will be clear and you will know what you are called to do.

After all, Jesus told us the Holy Spirit will guide, direct, teach, comfort, counsel, and show God's children what is going to happen in the future. Prayer is a conversation that will help our relationship grow. God is willing to speak to us through the Bible. Also, the Holy Spirit speaks to us through a small voice, and it's time for us to listen and obey God. I believe listening to God's voice is what is missing in many of God's children who do not know what abundant life in Christ is about.

After God asked me to spend 10 percent of my time in prayer every day, I started praying more, mostly talking. Then one day, while I was praying, I heard a clear voice from God that He wants to talk to me and I should be quiet and listen in silence. I was surprised because up to that time I acted as if praying is leaving a request in an answering machine. I did all the talking and I didn't give God any chance to talk.

I started to practice listening to God, and He started revealing things to me. I had many misconceptions and one of them was that if

I responded to a call to ministry, I had to do it on my own. All that was changed since God started revealing to me His heart and started changing my way of thinking. Prayer became a time to learn about God's heart and His passion.

My conversations with God through prayer have transformed my heart. I have received many spiritual blessings and learned lessons that prayer is a blessing in my spiritual journey. My prayer life has been enriched because God taught me how to listen.

Without growing in our relationship with the Lord, we will have an empty heart and we will feel something is still missing. Yes, many of us are missing out big time because we ignore the Lord when we pray. So, my prayer is that this prayer project will bring healing in your hearts especially in your relationship with the Lord so you will be able to listen to his clear voice.

1. Who needs this prayer?

This prayer is for anyone who want to learn how to listen to God's voice and to find God's plans for their lives. Jesus said, *"My sheep listen to my voice." (John 10:17, Hebrews 1:1)* Jesus seeks an intimate relationship with us and wants to speak to us; He wants to reveal His plans for our lives. People who do not hear or recognize God's voice are confused, lack vision, feel empty inside, and don't understand what God wants them to do with their lives. When we learn to listen and obey the plans that God reveals to us, we find purpose in life and fulfillment. Seeking Him with all our hearts is the key to listening: *"You will seek me and find me when you seek me with all your heart." (Jeremiah 29:13)*

Read the Bible for 30 minutes and pray for 30 minutes for the next 30 days. Don't give up this prayer because you don't hear immediately from God. Remember Solomon gave 1,000 offerings when God appealed to him in a dream and spoke to him. *(1 Kings 3:1 -15)* You have to be persistent in prayer if you want to hear from God. *(Matthew 7:7-8)*

2. How does God speak to us and what can we do to listen?

God has spoken audibly to people, but most of the time, He speaks to us through the Holy Spirit. The Holy Spirit reveals to us what God wants us to know: *"No eye has seen, no ear has heard, no mind has conceived what God has prepared for those who love Him – but God has revealed it to us by His Spirit." (1 Corinthians 2:9-10) "But the Counselor, the Holy Spirit, whom the Father will send in my name, will teach you all things and will remind you of everything I have said to you." (John 14:26) "When the Counselor comes, whom I will send to you from the Father, the Spirit of truth who goes out from the Father, he will testify about me." (John 15:26) "He will bring glory to me by taking from what is mine and making it known to you." (John 16:14)* The Holy Spirit helps us understand what Jesus is telling us. When we accept Jesus as our Lord and Savior, the Holy Spirit starts working in us and helps us to cultivate the gardens in our hearts, so we can understand what God wants us to do. The Holy Spirit can speak to our spirits with or without words and gives us spiritual understanding, wisdom, knowledge, and revelation, so we can understand God's heart. God's language is much broader than we can think or imagine. The Holy Spirit speaks to us in many ways.

(1) <u>God speaks to us through the words of the Bible</u>: Read the Bible 30 minutes every day for the next 30 days. The Holy Spirit uses Scripture to guide, convict, direct, comfort, counsel, and teach us. We need to study the Bible if we want God to direct our paths. When we go through trials, God uses the Scriptures to console and comfort us; and when He does this it confirms for us that God is with us, and this helps us grow in faith. *(John 14:15-17, 25-26, 15:26, 16:5-15)* The Holy Spirit helps us understand when we are spiritually empty and need to be filled with the Holy Spirit. The Word of God satisfies our spiritual hunger, and our spirit will know when God is near. Our spiritual hunger is something that Jesus understood when the devil tempted Him. He said, *"Man does not live on bread alone, but on every word that comes from the mouth of God." (Matthew 4:4)* Read Romans, John, Acts, Hosea, and other books of the Bible that have words that will help you listen to God. If you don't understand the Bible, pray: "Holy Spirit, bless me with wisdom, knowledge, understanding, and revelation, so I can understand the word of God and obey Him."

(2) <u>God speaks to us as we spend time in prayer</u>: Pray for 30 minutes every day (speaking to God for 15 minutes and listening to God

for 15 minutes): prayer is communication between God and us. Many people think it is only important to talk to God, but it is more important to wait, to be still before Him, and to listen. Invite Jesus to speak to you by saying: "Lord Jesus, please speak to me. I am listening. I love you." Clear your mind and listen in silence. Let go of your scattered thoughts; write down whatever comes to your mind. When God speaks to you, what you write will always agree with His written Word. Write down the questions you have for God; and when you have an answer to a question, write it down. It's not easy to clear your mind at first, but you will be able to do it if you keep practicing. Many times we do not receive spiritual blessings because we don't ask. During this prayer, add your personal prayer and count the days. If we are persistent, God will let us know that He will answer our prayers even before it happens. When He says "no" to our prayer request, we need to change our prayers. When Paul's prayer was not answered the way he wanted, God gave him the reason. *"But he said to me, 'My grace is sufficient for you, for my power is made perfect in weakness.' Therefore I will boast all the more gladly about my weaknesses, so that Christ's power may rest on me."* *(2 Corinthians 12:9)* <u>Prepare your heart through a prayer of surrender</u>: Throughout the day, whenever you can, pray this prayer: "Dear Jesus, I surrender my life and everything to you. Open my heart, so I can listen to your voice. I surrender all my plans because you have better plans for me. Break my hardened heart and work in me, so I can repent of all my sins. Forgive my sins and cleanse me, so that when you speak to me there will be no distractions. Jesus, I love you."

(3) <u>The Holy Spirit convicts us of our sin</u>: If you are living a sinful life, you need to repent and change your life. Forgive yourself and others. Bless and pray for others who have hurt you. Let go of all the resentment, anger, hate and bitterness you have in your heart. Without repentance, there is no forgiveness and no spiritual blessing. When Peter preached, he told others to repent, be baptized, and then they would be forgiven and receive the Holy Spirit. *(Acts 2:37-41, John 7:37-38, 8:31-32, 16:8-9)* Determine not to sin with your mouth: speak words that create peace, faith, and spiritual victory. Thank God for everything,

even the hard times. Anything you have told God that you would do, follow through with it. *(Philippians 4:4-8, Hebrews 12:14, Ephesians 4:17-32, 1 Peter 3:10-12)* If you want Jesus to answer your prayer, you need to have a relationship with Him. Invite Jesus into your heart and be saved. Here is a prayer you can pray: "Lord Jesus, I am a sinner. Forgive my sins. I give my heart to you. I surrender my life to you. Come into my heart and take control of my life. Fill me with the Holy Spirit and speak to me so I can obey you. In the name of Jesus, I pray. Amen"

(4) <u>The Holy Spirit speaks to us by giving us spiritual assignments</u>: The devil will try to tempt you to fall into sin, but the Holy Spirit will give you assignments to guide you to grow in faith and to help others grow in faith. Also, the Holy Spirit tests you to see if you will obey Him from time to time. Do whatever the Holy Spirit asks you to do, even the little things. When God can trust you that you are a faithful and trustworthy servant, you will be anointed to do the work of God. Jesus said, *"But you will receive power when the Holy Spirit comes on you; and you will be my witnesses in Jerusalem, and in all Judea and Samaria, and to the ends of the earth." (Acts 1:8, 10:9-23, 13:1-3, 16:10)* Not everyone experiences the Holy Spirit even though they say that they are believers. Jesus spent more than three years with His disciples, and yet He told them to wait for the Holy Spirit. For you who have not experienced the Holy Spirit's power in your life, spend an hour clearing your mind, learn to wait before God in silence for the next one or two weeks, and ask the Holy Spirit to speak to you. Practice this until you experience the Holy Spirit.

(5) <u>God makes His presence known to us as we worship and when we are in Bible studies and prayer circles</u>: These are holy times when God communicates with us, brings healing, and fills our hearts with unspeakable joy, peace, and love. The tears we often experience at such holy moments water the garden God is tending in our hearts. *(Acts 4:23-41)* In the book of Hosea, God compares our hearts to a garden. *"Judah must plow, and Jacob must break up the ground. Sow for yourselves righteousness, reap the fruit of unfailing love, and break up your unplowed ground; for it is time to seek the Lord, until he comes and*

showers righteousness on you. But you have planted wickedness, you have reaped evil, you have eaten the fruit of deception." (Hosea 10:11-13) Our hearts need to be broken before God, and we need to make the effort to plant the seed of righteousness in them. The sign of a broken heart is the tears we cry when we are in the presence of God. He blesses us with showers of tears as we spend time with Him. The Holy Spirit starts breaking the hard ground of our hearts, and we feel the presence of the Lord when we worship Him, or when God speaks to us with comforting words, or convicts us of our sin. Our tears are the evidence of that; however, not everyone will experience this special grace of the Holy Spirit. The Holy Spirit brings healing through our tears even though we might not know why we are crying. Spend time with those who are filled with the Holy Spirit, so you can learn from them. Attending worship, Bible study, prayer circles and holy conversations with others are important if you want to learn to hear from God. *(Acts 2:14-41)*

(6) <u>God can speak to us through dreams</u>: We need to ask God for interpretation of our dreams. The Holy Spirit gives us dreams to direct us and to help us understand our spiritual condition; they can also reveal something God wants us to know concerning our futures or the futures of our loved ones, so we will know what to pray. *(Acts 2:17, John 16:13)* For those who suffer from nightmares, read the Bible and pray more. The devil torments people by giving them nightmarish dreams, but prayer is powerful against him. Not all nightmares are from the devil, God can show us what is happening in our spiritual world, so we can pray.

(7) <u>God also speaks to us through visions</u>: He directs our spiritual path, or gives us understanding of what is happening in the spiritual world, or tells us what is going to happen in the future. *(Acts 2:17, Acts 27:23-25)* Write your visions or images and ask for an interpretation. God may communicate with you through visions, and some spiritual visions come with images in your mind. The devil can also give you visions and images in your mind which will lead you to ungodly thoughts and destructive behaviors. Resist any ungodly thoughts and images and focus your heart and mind on Christ by meditating on the Scriptures.

Pray for wisdom and discernment to know the difference. *(James 1:1-18, 3:13-18)*

(8) <u>The Holy Spirit speaks to us through other mature Christians' teaching, preaching, writing, and testimonies</u>: Paul has helped many to grow in faith throughout many generations because of the letters that he wrote while in prison. God can use us regardless of our circumstances and will anoint us to do the work of God if we are willing to obey Him.

(9) <u>A Spiritual Journal can help us to listen to God's voice</u>: Write any questions you might have and ask the Lord to speak to you. Then, quite your mind in silence and write down what He may be speaking to you. As you start writing how God has helped you, the Holy Spirit can tell you the things that you need to know. God speaks to us through hardships and circumstances. Through reflection, God can reveal to us what He wants to teach us. Paul had hardships and he understood that through his suffering he learned to rely on God for comfort, no one else. He also learned that God can help him to comfort and encourage others even though he was going through suffering. That's God's grace. *(2 Corinthians 1:3-11, Philippians 4:8)*

3. <u>It is crucial to discern the voices you hear.</u>

(1) <u>Our mind is a spiritual battlefield</u>: There are four voices we hear in our minds: 1) the voice of the Holy Spirit; 2) the voice of the devil; 3) the voice of other people; 4) our own voices. The voice of the Holy Spirit is positive, and listening to it helps us grow in faith. Until you obey Him, you will have a restless heart. However, as soon as you obey His voice, peace will fill your heart. On the other hand, the voice of the devil is negative, critical, ungodly, hurtful, and destructive. The devil always makes sin appealing so that people fall into sin and lose peace.

(2) <u>What to do when you hear destructive voices and see visions that leads to destruction</u>: The devil can speak to us with an audible voice, but mostly speaks to us in our minds. Some people hear voices telling them to hurt themselves and others. Also, the devil can give us visions and images that will lead us to sin and destruction. Rebuke it: "In the name of Jesus, spirit of lies, destruction, and torment, leave me. I am covered by the blood of

Jesus. I am a child of God and I am going to serve Jesus."
Whenever you have destructive thoughts, hear voices, or see
visions that are not from God, pray the Lord's Prayer again and
again, especially the part: "Deliver us from evil."

(3) The Word of God has spiritual power: We can be strong as we
read the Bible and pray for healing of our minds. I believe many
people who hurt themselves and others or who commit suicide
are the victims of destructive voices and were tormented inside
their minds and didn't know how to resist the devil. Many who
hear voices have gone through traumatic events in their lives, and
they need healing. If you hear destructive voices, forgive others
and forgive yourself. Prayer: "Lord Jesus, because you have
forgiven me, died on the cross, and shed your blood for my sins, I
forgive myself and forgive others who have hurt me. I bless
others who have hurt me. Heal my wounds and my painful
memories and fill my heart with your love, peace and joy. Help
me to serve you." Jesus was tempted by the devil to jump off a
high building and kill himself, but he won the battle with the
Word of God. So can you resist the devil's temptation with God's
Word. *(Luke 1:1-13) "The Spirit of the Lord is on me, because he
has anointed me to preach good news to the poor. He has sent me
to proclaim freedom for the prisoners and recovery of sight for
the blind, to release the oppressed, to proclaim the year of the
Lord's favor." (Luke 4:18-19)*

(4) God has plans for you: Don't ignore what God is trying to tell
you. You need to understand what His plan is in order for you to
be productive in God's kingdom building business. So, ask the
Lord what you need to do to serve Him because He knows what
you need to do to be fruitful. *"'For I know the plans I have for
you,' declares the Lord, 'Plans to prosper you and not to harm
you, plans to give you hope and a future. Then you will call upon
me and come and pray to me, and I will listen to you. You will
seek me and find me when you seek me with all your heart. I will
be found by you,' declares the Lord, 'and will bring you back
from captivity.'" (Jeremiah 29:11-14)* God gave you the gift of
life so you can use it to help others. Volunteer to help others in
the community, church or in a mission. *"Then Jesus came to
them and said, "All authority in heaven and on earth has been*

given to me. Therefore go and make disciples of all nations, baptizing them in the name of the Father and of the Son and of the Holy Spirit, and teaching them to obey everything I have commanded you. And surely I am with you always, to the very end of the age." (Matthew 29:18-20) Prayer: "God enlarge my vision and mission to serve you and others. Open the doors that I will be able to make many disciples of Jesus and to help others who are hurting to bring healing with your help."

3. A Victory Prayer

Write your prayers of victory

What we proclaim in Christ will make a difference in our spiritual journey in the long run and it will affect us while we are awake or asleep. Claiming victory in Christ shows that we do believe in God's power to overcome all our difficulties. We need to claim the big picture which God has created for us to have victories and abundant life. We can envision our future with hope and peace with words and in faith. Sometimes traumatic events in our lives take away the peace and joy we are promised in Christ. This can hinder us from seeing the victorious picture that God wants us to see.

I wrote a prayer of victory to be healed from anxiety attacks. Whenever the spirits of fear and anxiety try to take over my mind, I claim victory in Christ. This prayer has helped me immensely and I have not had an anxiety attack since I started proclaiming victory. Write your own prayer of victory and start proclaiming victory in your life. Here is the victory prayer I wrote:

1. A victory prayer for myself

I claim victory that I made a decision to love Jesus.
He is the first priority in my life.
I claim victory for God because He has the ultimate power
over everything in my life, no one else does.
I claim victory for making a commitment to serve Christ.
I claim victory over my guilt and shame so that all my sins are
washed away by the blood of Jesus Christ
I claim victory that God is the source of my love, peace,
wisdom, joy, and strength.
I claim victory over my future belief that
God is going to bless me beyond my imagination.
I claim victory because I decided to love Jesus more than my
sinful desires and passion.
I claim victory over all my problems and concerns
so that I am continuously surrendering everything to God.
I claim victory that I made a decision to bless and forgive those
who have hurt me.

I claim victory over my fears because God is guiding
my spiritual path.
I claim victory over my life challenges knowing that
God is going to give me wisdom to handle it.

2. A victory prayer for my family
I claim victory that God will take care of my family
for His glory.
I claim victory that my family will be filled with
the Holy Spirit and serve God to the fullest.
I claim victory that God will give my children spiritual
blessings beyond my imagination.
I claim victory for my children that God will provide what
they need, including godly mentors.
I claim victory that my family will be blessed with
spiritual gifts and use them for God's glory.
I claim victory that God will take care of my family
when I cannot take care of them.
I claim victory that God will protect my family and
help them grow in faith.
I claim victory that other people will be blessed by
my family's presence and ministry.

3. A victory prayer for my ministry
I claim victory that God will provide an opportunity
for me to spread the gospel of Jesus much more than
I have ever imagined.
I claim victory that with God's help, I will be able to help
others use their spiritual gifts to the maximum for God's glory.
I claim victory that the Holy Spirit will bring powerful
Christian leaders to join me in building up the kingdom
of God to win many lost souls and grow spiritually.
I claim victory that God will help me use my time wisely
to reach out to those who are in spiritual bondage,
so they can find spiritual freedom in Christ.

I claim victory because I am continuously surrendering
all my plans and desires in order to love and serve Christ.
I claim victory in managing financial resources with God's
wisdom so that I will glorify God with my resources and help
others to be saved and find hope and healing in Christ.
I claim victory that the Holy Spirit will anoint me so much that
others will experience the Holy Spirit's healing presence
through my ministry and book projects.
I claim victory that when God has different ministry plans for
my life, I will obey Him because His plans are always better
than mine.
I claim victory over my selfishness that I will look after Jesus'
interest, knowing that it is the only way to build up Christ's
kingdom.
I claim victory because I will be focusing all my gifts, time,
energy on loving Jesus and serving Him to the fullest.

Part Six:
An Invitation

1. AN INVITATION TO ACCEPT CHRIST – Words of Invitation from the F Module Pod 1300 and Prayer Written by D Module Pod 5 Maximum Saints from the ACDF.

Are you questioning God? Do you lift your hands in frustration and cry? Have you created an unbearable amount of pain in your life that you cannot handle? Are loved ones on the outside reaching out to you, but they can no longer touch you? Is there an incredible emptiness and pain in your stomach that no one understands? A pain that no one can take away? No more questioning: Now is the time to act! Do not delay!! Bow down. Let the One who created the world lift your burdens and cleanse your soul. Let Jesus' love, hope and joy fill you to the maximum. Jesus can help you deal with pain when no one else can. He can give you peace when no one else can. Here is a prayer that you can pray (if you would like to invite Christ into your heart), so you can be saved and experience the peace of Christ in your heart.

Prayer: "Dear Jesus, I am prepared to invite you into my heart, mind, body and soul. I come before you offering myself as a living sacrifice, confessing my sins and weaknesses. Father, I put all of my trust in you and I want You to have total control over my life. I am sorry, Lord, for the things I have done that grieve you and others. Please forgive me for all of my sins. I ask that the distractions around me be put on hold so that I will be able to receive you into my life today. Please send your Holy Spirit into my heart and give me the power to live a new life in Christ. Thank you, Lord, for your love. I give my life to you in the name of Jesus. Amen"

"If you confess with your mouth, 'Jesus is Lord,' and believe in your heart that God raised Him from the dead you will be saved." (Romans 10:9) "If we confess our sins, he is faithful and just and will forgive us our sins and purify us from all unrighteousness." (1 John 1:9) "Jesus answered, 'I am the way and the truth and the life. No one comes to the Father except through me." (John 14:6)

2. An Invitation for The Transformation Project Prison Ministry (TPPM):

Books and DVDs produced by TPPM are distributed in many jails, prisons and homeless shelters nationwide free of charge made possible by grants and donations. America has 2.3 million people incarcerated, the largest prison population in the world. There is a great shortage of inspirational books in many jails and prisons.

"One Million Dream Project"

In 2010, TPPM board decided to expand the ministry goal, and started the "One Million Dream Project." TPPM decided to raise enough funds to distribute one million copies of each book that TPPM has produced for prisoners and homeless people. I ask you to pray for this project so God can help TPPM to reach out to those who cannot speak for themselves and are in need of spiritual guidance.

TPPM is a 501(c)(3) nonprofit organization, so your donation is 100% tax deductible. If you would like to be a partner in this very important mission of bringing transformation through the message of Christ in prisons and homeless shelters, or want to know more about this project, please visit our website: www.maximumsaints.org. You can donate on line or you can write a check addressed to:

Transformation Project Prison Ministry
5209 Montview Boulevard
Denver, CO 80207

Website: www.maximumsaints.org
Facebook: http://tinyurl.com/yhhcp5g

3. How to Purchase *Maximum Saints* Books:

This is for individuals who would like to purchase or send a copy to their incarcerated family. TPPM receives lots of requests for individual distribution but we only distribute them through chaplains. All the proceeds from *Maximum Saints* will go to TPPM to distribute more free books and DVDs to prisons and homeless shelters.

To find out more about purchasing *Maximum Saints* books, check our website: www.maximumsaints.org. The following books are available:

Book One: *Maximum Saints Never Hide in the Dark*
Book Two: *Maximum Saints Make No Little Plans*
Book Three: *Maximum Saints Dream*
Book Four: *Maximum Saints Forgive*
Book Five: *Maximum Saints All Things Are Possible*

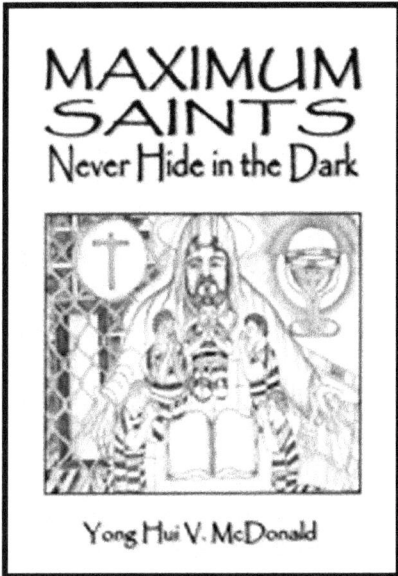

MAXIMUM
SAINTS
Never Hide in the Dark

Yong Hui V. McDonald

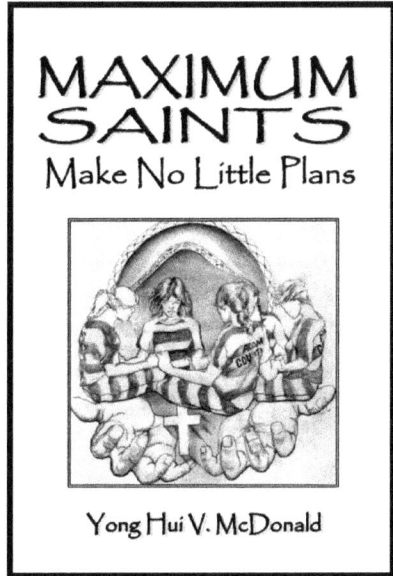

MAXIMUM
SAINTS
Make No Little Plans

Yong Hui V. McDonald

MAXIMUM SAINTS DREAM

Yong Hui V. McDonald

MAXIMUM SAINTS FORGIVE

Yong Hui V. McDonald

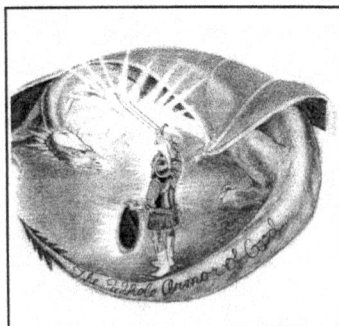

MAXIMUM SAINTS All Things Are Possible

Yong Hui V. McDonald

ABOUT THE AUTHOR

Yong Hui V. McDonald, also known as Vescinda McDonald, is a chaplain at Adams County Detention Facility, certified American Correctional Chaplain, spiritual director and on-call hospital chaplain. She founded the Transformation Project Prison Ministry (TPPM) in 2005 and founded GriefPathway Ventures, LLC in 2010 to help others learn how to process grief and healing. She also is the founder of Veterans Twofish Foundation, a 501(c)(3) non-profit, in 2011.

Education:
- Multnomah Bible College, B.A.B.E. (1984)
- Iliff School of Theology, Master of Divinity (2002)
- The Samaritan Counseling & Educational Center, Clinical Pastoral Education (CPE) (2002)
- Rocky Mountain Pastoral Care and Training Center (CPE) (2003)
- Formation Program for Spiritual Directors (2004)
- Rocky Mountain Center for Education and Training, CPE (2011)

Books and Audio books by Yong Hui V. McDonald:
- *Moment by Moment*
- *Journey With Jesus, Visions, Dreams, Meditations & Reflections*
- *Dancing in the Sky, A Story of Hope for Grieving Hearts*
- *Twisted Logic, The Shadow of Suicide*
- *Twisted Logic, The Window of Depression*
- *Dreams & Interpretations, Healing from Nightmares*
- *I Was The Mountain, In Search of Faith & Revival*
- *The Ultimate Parenting Guide, How to Enjoy Peaceful Parenting and Joyful Children*
- *Prisoners Victory Parade, Extraordinary Stories of Maximum Saints & Former Prisoners*
- *Four Voices, How They Affect Our Minds: How to Overcome Self-Destructive Voices and Hear the Nurturing Voice of God*
- *Tornadoes, Lessons, Teachings: How to Rise Above Grief, Loss, Trauma, and PTSD Using the TLT Model*
- Compiled and published five *Maximum Saints* books under the Transformation Project Prison Ministry.

DVDs produced by Yong Hui:
- *Dancing in The Sky, Mismatched Shoes*
- *Tears of The Dragonfly, Suicide and Suicide Prevention (CD* is also available*)*

Spanish books produced by Yong Hui:
- *Twisted Logic, The Shadow of Suicide*
- *Journey With Jesus, Visions, Dreams, Meditations & Reflections*

GriefPathway Ventures, LLC.
P.O. Box 220
Brighton, CO 80601
Website: www.griefpathway.com
Email: griefpwv@gmail.com

www.ingramcontent.com/pod-product-compliance
Lightning Source LLC
Chambersburg PA
CBHW060805050426
42449CB00008B/1545